INDIA IN TRANSITION

INDIA IN TRANSITION

Issues of Political Economy in a Plural Society

F. Tomasson Jannuzi

Westview Press
BOULDER, SAN FRANCISCO, & LONDON

Westview Special Studies on South and Southeast Asia

This Westview softcover edition is printed on acid-free paper and bound in softcovers that carry the highest rating of the National Association of State Textbook Administrators, in consultation with the Association of American Publishers and the Book Manufacturers' Institute.

Copyright © 1989 by Westview Press, Inc.

Published in 1989 in the United States of America by Westview Press, Inc., 5500 Central Avenue, Boulder, Colorado 80301, and in the United Kingdom by Westview Press, Inc., 13 Brunswick Centre, London WC1N 1AF, England

Library of Congress Cataloging-in-Publication Data
Jannuzi, F. Tomasson. 1934–
   India in transition : issues of political economy in a plural
   society / by F. Tomasson Jannuzi.
   p.   cm.—(Westview special studies on South and Southeast
   Asia)
   Includes index.
   ISBN 0-8133-7723-4
   1. India—Economic policy—1980–   . 2. India—Economic
conditions—1947–   . I. Title. II. Series.
HC435.2.J358 1989
320.954—dc19   88-39689
                                                                      CIP

Printed and bound in the United States of America

The paper used in this publication meets the requirements of the American National Standard for Permanence of Paper for Printed Library Materials Z39.48-1984.

10   9   8   7   6   5   4   3   2   1

For

Barbara

CONTENTS

PREFACE

I believe that it should be standard in the social sciences for an author to identify the personal valuations and assumptions that condition or qualify his work. By this means he can give his readers a sense of his motivation and biases, providing them a basis for interpreting the context that informs the work. What follows is my attempt to enable readers to trace the origins of my approach and arguments.

The essay derives in part from my peculiar experience in the field of "Indian Studies" over more than thirty years -- roughly from 1954 to the present, 1988. From my undergraduate days at Dartmouth College in the 1950s, I have been intrigued with the problems and prospects of The Republic of India. The precise origins of my interest in India are obscure. But, it is significant to me that my interest was already so deeply defined in 1954 (when I was nineteen years of age) that I sought and secured a fellowship at Dartmouth that would permit me to spend my senior year in independent study and research on India.

That fellowship gave me a competitive edge in securing in 1955 one of a limited number of Foreign Area Fellowships sponsored by the Ford Foundation. My fellowship, consistent with my own design, supported me for several years of study in Britain (at the London School of Economics and the School of Oriental and African Studies) and field research in India. Given my interest in India, my primary alternative to graduate study in Britain at that time would have been to matriculate at the University of Pennsylvania, where W. Norman Brown had initiated in 1946 what was then widely perceived to be the only significant American program in South Asian studies. At the time, I recall rejecting even the notion of applying for admission at Pennsylvania because my incipient interests in India were already focused on contemporary issues of development and political economy, rather than on what I presumed to be the classical civilization emphasis at Pennsylvania. Even then the challenge of India for me had to do mainly with its developmental aspirations and dreams for the future, and not with the history of its great civilizations.

In London I was drawn progressively away from the intellectual emphases at the School of Oriental and African Studies to those of the London School of Economics and Political Science. That is to say, in an elemental sense, I became more preoccupied with the hopes and aspirations of those who were concerned with modern India than with the focus of those who concentrated on the British Raj and the richness of India's historical traditions; indeed, "the wonder that was India."[1]

The prime stimulus in this was the inspired teaching and scholarship of the late Vera Anstey of the London School of Economics. No one could work closely with Vera Anstey without being profoundly influenced. It was she -- together with some already venerated "old India hands" with whom she maintained close ties, Sir Malcolm Darling and Harold Mann -- who first encouraged me to design a program of field research in India that would be rooted in the countryside, rather than in academic or governmental institutions.

For Anstey, Darling, and Mann, the future of India would be determined by poor peasants, rather than by a few leaders drawn from the urban, educated, English-speaking elite who were then a conspicuous part of the British colonial legacy. For them, unlike those whose definition of economic progress was largely urban and

---

1. The phrase quoted draws consciously from the distinguished work by this title by A.L. Basham -- a member of the faculty of the School of Oriental and African Studies when I was enrolled there in 1955.

industrial,[2] it was obvious that the economic development of India would have to be based on an agricultural revolution that conferred hope, increased opportunity, and new dignity to India's rural majority. For them, India's future was dependent less on whether British-inspired parliamentary institutions took hold and were ritualistically perpetuated than on the ability of the newly independent state to deliver the mass of the people out of poverty.

While never preaching the point, Anstey, Darling and Mann demonstrated in their behavior and orientation a belief that India's independence and political freedom would be without much substance if its rural majority did not experience personally the benefits of economic emancipation. I came to share their view.

Therefore, it is not surprising that, when I finally encountered India first-hand in 1956, I eschewed living in an urban area, did not rely on data on rural India generated by the Planning Commission in New Delhi, and attempted both to establish my own nexus with the people in the countryside and to gather, however imperfectly, my own data. In this enterprise, aided by a friend, Dayanand Sahay, who had been associated with Jaya Prakash Narayan, I had my initiation to India in rural Bihar.[3]

---

2. The initial emphasis in India's development plans was in the promotion of "heavy industries." The basic model, designed in the Soviet Union as early as 1928, was elaborated in India by Professor P.C. Mahalanobis. [See, for example, P.C. Mahalanobis, "Science and National Planning," Sankhya, *The Indian Journal of Statistics*, Vol. 20, Parts 1 & 2, (September 1958), p. 85.]

3. My interest in rural development issues was further stimulated by meetings in Patna in 1956-57 with Jaya Prakash Narayan, the distinguished socialist leader, whose last prominence in India (before he died) was in the context of his mobilization of opposition to the authority of Prime Minister Indira Gandhi and the Congress (I) in the 1970s. My early meetings with "J.P.," as he was known to those around him, were intriguing because they occurred at a pivotal moment in his life, when he had decided to leave politics (his active association with the Praja Socialist Party) to become a follower of Vinobha Bhave and the *Bhoodan* (land-gift) movement (perceived by some at the time to be a credible, apolitical means of providing land to the landless in rural India). As "J.P." sought to rationalize his new course, he attracted a number

(continued...)

Why Bihar? I was intrigued then as I am now with the fact that Bihar is synonymous with economic and political backwardness in modern India, yet was both the home of advanced civilizations in ancient India and peculiarly blessed in its modern economic potential (with rich soil, a high water table, and an unusual spectrum of natural resources). If this state, with a potential for economic progress greater than that of the Punjab, could not be transformed economically, which state could?

My immersion in Bihar, my exposure to what can be described as a traditional agrarian economy and its local critics (especially friends in the Praja Socialist Party, and Jaya Prakash Narayan), had a decisive influence in shaping my perceptions of some of the problems of modern India. My first-hand encounters with landlords, or *zamindars*, who exercised semi-feudal control over the people in the countryside, my experience within a largely pre-market or command economy, my sense of the powerlessness of people without land in an agrarian society -- all these things were products of my time in Bihar. None of the reading on India I had done had equipped me adequately for that experience. I was shocked and angered by what I saw in Bihar in 1956-1957 -- by the elemental violence meted out customarily to poor peasants within the framework and hierarchical traditions of the zamindari system, and by the then seeming acquiescence of the people to the power and prerogatives of those above them in the agrarian hierarchy. I was also greatly moved by the dignity and wisdom of the rural poor, and their willingness to reach out to me in ways that conferred some acceptance, despite puzzlement at my presence and purposes.

Though I have lived for extended periods in South India and New Delhi in the 1960s,[4] and travelled

---

3(...continued)

of gifted persons to his counsel, among them the distinguished economists M.L. Dantwala and the late Raj Krishna. Both of these men also made deep impressions on me at the time because of their evident interest in devising development strategies that would contribute to the well-being of peasants.

4. In South India, in what was then the state of Mysore, my wife and I

(continued...)

extensively throughout the country in the 1970s and 1980s, my perceptions of India are to some degree not detached from my early experience within the political economy of Bihar in the 1950s. This means that I must consciously strive in my teaching at The University of Texas at Austin and in my research not to be imprisoned within that early experience -- extrapolating unconsciously from it to reach broader conclusions than might be warranted about India as a whole. In this respect, I consider myself no different than other Americans of my generation who became engaged in Indian studies. It seems to me that we all work within the framework of insights that are particularistic within initial experience, even as we strive over time to broaden our perceptions -- daring at times even to believe that we have established some basis for generalizations about a society as complex and as diverse as India's.

F. Tomasson Jannuzi

4(...continued)

worked at a rural development training center in the days when the national panacea for transforming India's agrarian sector was "Community Development." In New Delhi, we were representatives of an American foundation which, with the approval of the Government of India, contributed impetus to the development of a variety of indigenous educational institutions: for example, the "Centre for the Study of Developing Societies" in Delhi and the "Institute for Constitutional and Parliamentary Studies" in New Delhi.

ACKNOWLEDGMENTS

I am indebted to my family, friends, professional colleagues and students in India, the United States, and Britain who have made my life a continuing seminar in the field of "Indian and South Asian Studies" over the last thirty-two years. It would be inappropriate to single out some for special mention while, inevitably, omitting many others. To them collectively I owe thanks for whatever meaningful insights I have concerning the political economy of India. However, it is I who assumes full responsibility for the actual contents of this essay.

INTRODUCTION

In this book I am making some generalizations about contemporary India and the years immediately ahead -- daring to set forth some of my personal concerns for critical review by those in the United States and in India who share in varying degrees my concern for India's future. I am writing with empathy for those who presently govern India -- those who, unlike me, have an inescapable daily responsibility to wrestle with the intertwined political and economic problems of so complex and plural a society. I am writing with appreciation of the magnitude of India's commitment, as articulated in its Constitution and its Five Year Plans, to nothing less than a social and economic revolution to be achieved peacefully within democratic institutions. But, I am writing also with the awareness that a vast gap persists in India, forty-one years after independence from Britain, between the national goals first articulated and actual achievements, however measured. The existence of such a gap should be expected by anyone who recognizes that no level of achievement in modern India could possibly have been sufficient to meet rising expectations within a society whose population has more than doubled since independence. On the other hand, the gap between articulated goals and what has been delivered to the people as a whole cannot be ignored by anyone who believes that efforts to close that gap must be persistent if the Republic of India is to remain a viable entity.

The book is rooted in the assumption that India is a plural society. At one level, this suggests an obvious recognition of India's great diversity of peoples and particularlistic interests.   Moreover, I am using the term "plural society" within the definitional frame established long ago by J.S. Furnivall.   Furnivall   said that such a society was comprised of "... two or more elements or social orders which live side by side, yet without mingling, in one political unit."[1]   He also said that, in such a society,

> ... there is no common will except, possibly, in matters of supreme importance, such as resistance to aggression from outside.   In its political aspect a plural society resembles a confederation of allied provinces, united by treaty or within the limits of a formal constitution, merely for some ends common to the constituent units and, in matters outside the terms of union, each living its own life. But it differs from a confederation in that the constituent elements are not segregated each within its own territorial limits.   In a confederation secession is at least possible without the total disruption of all social bonds, whereas in a plural society the elements are so intermingled that secession is identical with anarchy.   Thus a plural society has the instability of a confederation, but without the remedy which is open to a confederation if the yoke of common union should become intolerable.[2]

Extending his discussion to the sphere of economics in the plural society, Furnivall introduced the concept of social demand. He said that in a plural society there was an absence of any common social demand because there was a lack of common will. Added Furnivall,

---

1. Furnivall, J.S. *Netherlands India: A Study of Plural Economy.* (Cambridge: Cambridge University Press, 1944), p. 446.

2. Ibid., p. 447.

The conception of social demand has received less attention from economists than it would seem to merit. Adam Smith and his successors, urging the doctrines of individualism and freedom of enterprise as the mainspring of wealth, took for granted the existence and efficacy of social demand; in the circumstances of the time, and especially in England with its conservative traditions and its stable institutions, social demand could safely be ignored. ... But, in a plural society, social demand is disorganized; social wants are sectional, and there is no social demand common to all the several elements. ... This disorganization of social demand in a plural society has far-reaching effects; it is the root cause of all those properties which differentiate plural economy, the political economy of a plural society, from unitary economy, the political economy of a homogeneous society.[3]

And Furnivall concluded,

In every community there is a conflict of interest between town and country, industry and agriculture, capital and labour; but the asperity of conflict is softened by a common citizenship. ... But, in a plural society the basic problem ... is far more elemental; it is impossible to provide a vehicle for the expression of social will until there is a society capable of will, and the basic problem ... in such a community is the integration of society.[4]

If India is indeed a plural society of the sort described by Furnivall, then it follows that economic development in such a society must be sought by some means in addition to a favorable growth rate sustained over time. Economic

---

3. Ibid., p. 449.

4. Ibid., p. 463.

development in such a society requires the building of a progressively more integrated social and economic system. In the case of India it requires the building of a society in which people evolve a sense of community, a *consensus universalis* that bridges the divisions imposed by language, by caste, by religion and economic privilege -- the opposite of what appears to be happening in contemporary India. Tarlok Singh, writing in retirement following many years on the Planning Commission of the Government of India, reached the same conclusion. He said that "economic development is but a means to an end -- the building up ... of a society without caste, class or privilege, which offers to every section of the community and to all parts of the country the fullest opportunity to grow and to contribute to the national well-being."[6]

Given such a perception of economic development, India's progress since Independence becomes less substantial than statistical indices might suggest -- less worthy of acclaim. The vision of an integrated Indian society seems distant, even Utopian. Yet, this vision, articulated by Indians themselves, remains a critical part of what India must be about in the interests of its own viability as a nation-state. Giving tangible expression to such a grand vision in any society is not the work of a few leaders and a few Five Year Plans. It must be the work of a whole people -- including "concerned outsiders" -- who learn in time to share the dream.

---

5. Alexis de Tocqueville used the term *consensus universalis* to refer to the manner in which America, even when engaged in tumultuous agitation on many issues, had established "... a tacit agreement and a sort of *consensus universalis* ..." concerning the republican principle embedded in its system of governance. [de Toqueville, Alexis. *Democracy in America*. Mayer, J.P. and Max Lerner, eds. A New Translation by George Lawrence. (New York, Evanston and London: Harper and Row, Publishers, 1966), p. 365.] I am using *consensus universalis* in the same spirit, emphasing the need for disparate groups in India's plural society to establish "tacit agreement" on themes that unify, themes that might supercede divisive issues.

6. Singh, Tarlok. *Towards an Integrated Society: Reflections on Planning, Social Policy and Rural Institutions*. (Westport, Connecticut: Greenwood Publishing Corporation, 1969), p. viii.

I am one of those concerned outsiders. Experience, training and empathy, if not nationality or citizenship, bind me to the articulated dreams of modern India's Founding Fathers, especially those linked to promises in documents of state and the various Five Year Plans to work toward the institutionalization of economic progress within a progressive, more egalitarian society. I have taken personal pride in India's achievements and in India's repeated demonstrations of resiliency, even in the face of problems that would test the mettle of any state, including a relatively rich one like the United States. I have been part of an informal lobby of Americans who have strived consciously to "interpret" India in the United States -- often with a view toward offsetting ignorant and crude stereotypes. I have written in critical terms about the political economy of India in the past -- emphasizing the gap between articulated goals and practical achievements. Now, I write in the spirit of critical concern about India's future -- a concern that the Indian people may now lose sight of the promises that they have made to themselves and thereby deny themselves the full fruits of their own labors to establish a modern political economy within which even the weakest sections of the peasantry have voices that are heard and in which a common will permeates the compartments of an otherwise plural society.

1

THE STYLE AND SUBSTANCE OF RAJIV GANDHI'S REGIME

If progress in India, as defined by Indians themselves, must ultimately imply the establishment of a *consensus universalis* based on common definitions of social and economic purpose, it is tempting to assign responsibility to a supreme leader for giving effective expression to those elusive common purposes that could provide unifying national identity. Such a delegation of responsibility is especially seductive in a plural society because it obviates the need throughout the society to expose, debate, and resolve the issues that at once define the society's pluralism and threaten national unity. In its essence, therefore, the practice is escapist.

Such a practice places extraordinary and unreasonable demands on the person who is designated from time to time to be the supreme leader. It makes him or her virtually the anthropomorphic incarnation of the "nation," and invests in the leader unique attributes and symbolic powers. Such a practice -- borne of what I believe to be unwitting escapism -- has been at work in India for some time. It is a practice of high risk, especially in a plural society that claims to be a participatory democracy. As the practice evolves, it subtly erodes peoples' confidence in their individual and collective capacities to address and resolve divisive issues. At the same time, it assigns responsibilities to the leader of the moment that are inherently unfair-- ignoring in the case of India the constitutional limits on leaders' powers while denying them the frailties inherent in the human condition.

While it is a primary theme of this work that we should not invest the leader of India with powers and responsibilities that are bound to exceed his capacities, this is not to suggest that the recognized and elected leader either does not matter or can be ignored. Accordingly, in this chapter I find it useful to examine briefly the style and substance of the regime of India's contemporary leader, Prime Minister Rajiv Gandhi. Nothing in this chapter, however, will obviate the need in subsequent chapters for analysis of issues in comtemporary India that places the leader in the context of a plural society -- an environment that will either constrict his areas of choice or free him to act in ways consistent with his own propensities.

PERCEPTIONS ROOTED IN SOUTH ASIA

Rajiv's Quick Rise

With the death of Sanjay Gandhi in 1980, many assumed that Prime Minister Indira Gandhi would not have time to groom a successor from within the "family." Even as late as October, 1984, it was not certain that her eldest son, Rajiv, would secure the support he needed when the time came to succeed his mother and to become the Prime Minister of India.[1] As it turned out, any questions concerning Rajiv Gandhi's capacity to succeed Mrs. Gandhi, or concerning his willingness even to commit himself to politics, were swept aside by the assassination of the Indian Prime Minister. No other scenario than the assassination could have ensured the quick and relatively

---

1. In the early Autumn of 1984, there was even the question whether Mrs. Gandhi would succeed herself in elections anticipated at the end of 1984 or early in 1985. As Mark Tully and Satish Jacob have suggested: "By 1984 her reputation had slumped ... Unrest over illegal immigration in the north-eastern state of Assam had been allowed to drift to disaster with three thousand people being massacred in an election Mrs. Gandhi forced on the Assamese people. ... By-elections were going badly for Mrs. Gandhi's Congress in spite of her son Rajiv's attempts to revive her party." [Tully, Mark, and Satish Jacob. *Amritsar: Mrs. Gandhi's Last Battle*. (London: Pan Books Ltd., 1986), pp. 13-14.]

easy process by which her son would be acclaimed the leader of the Congress Party and the new leader of India.

The very nature of Rajiv Gandhi's emergence as a national leader caused millions of people in India to invest in him their hopes for new beginnings. His subsequent success in the General Elections (however interpreted in detail) gave concrete expression to peoples' yearnings for a stable and prosperous future in which divisive issues would be resolved and tensions reduced. Even those in India who had been bitter and unforgiving critics of Indira Gandhi and her policies seemed willing in 1985 to accept Rajiv Gandhi's leadership -- giving him an unusual opportunity to establish his own course, free of the obligation to defend many of the programs and policies of his mother.[2]

---

2. It must be remembered that Indira Gandhi had numerous critics outside of the Punjab. Within days of her death, for example, the *Economic and Political Weekly*, on November 3, 1984, published an extraordinary editorial denouncing her legacy. An excerpt follows: "When she took charge two decades ago, she found a reasonably well-organized Congress party with several layers of responsive leadership across the length and breadth of the country. She dismantled the party and she did so with a clear purposiveness. Because she did not trust anyone who would not play a subservient role to her and her family, she got rid of the intermediate leadership and re-built the party as a paper entity, without a democratic structure and with office-bearers personally selected and named by her. In the process she alienated the political community as a whole, and in fact took malicious pleasure in exposing their follies and foibles. The outcome was inevitable. Today those with a reasonable span of administrative and political experience are nowhere near the proximity of power and responsibility in the Congress (I) party, and those who are placed in the administration in crucial positions are wanting in sagacity, competence and experience. The annihilation of a life is always a sad episode. But this fractured nation has now to fend for itself, and try to explore ways and means of extracting itself from the bondage of the inheritance of the past twenty years." [Quoted from "Indira Gandhi's Bequest." *Economic and Political Weekly*, Vol. XIX No.44. p. 1850.] Indira Gandhi's legacy remains controversial. Her detractors in India still criticize her for destroying the powers of state chief ministers, for weakening the federal structure, for diminishing the independence of the Indian judiciary, for questioning the quality of the civil service and for

(continued...)

However, attempts to provide "instant analysis" of the Indian General Elections in December of 1984 produced judgments that made too much of questionable data. I am skeptical about the sufficiency of various initial analyses of the dynamics of the 1984 elections, especially those which suggested that the elections signified some form of "Hindu revivalism" in the wake of Mrs. Gandhi's assassination by Sikhs. The following quotation from Robin Jeffrey's *What's Happening to India?* seems typical of early assessments. "In the national elections, large sections of north Indian Hindus seem to have been swept along by a novel sense of Hindu-ness, of Hindu unity. Usually divided by caste and class, now briefly at least, a wider identification appears to have influenced them."[3] Similar observations were advanced by Rajni Kothari in the *Guardian Weekly* in January of 1985 and by Myron Weiner during his participation in February 1985 in a symposium ("India 2000: The Next Fifteen Years") conducted by The Center for Asian Studies at The University of Texas at Austin. While it is well substantiated that the Congress Party (I) appealed to what Pranay Gupte has called "the deep-rooted communal instincts of India's Hindu majority",[4] particularly in Uttar Pradesh, Haryana, Bihar, Madhya Pradesh and parts of Rajasthan, it still seems inappropriate, even in 1988, to suggest that the 1984 elections were driven mainly by a phenomenon that can be classified as "Hindu revivalism."

Similarly, too much was made of the magnitude of the Congress Party's victory in the 1984 elections. While the numbers were undoubtedly impressive (the Congress won an unprecedented 401 out of 508 seats contested), the nature

---

2(...continued)

hurting its morale, for manipulating promotions in the army and using it for political purposes against civilians, and for turning the cabinet into a joke by vesting extraordinary power in her secretariat and her sons.

3. Jeffrey, Robin. *What's Happening to India?* (London: The Macmillan Press Ltd., 1986), p. 18.

4. Gupte, Pranay. *Vengeance: India After the Assassination of Indira Gandhi.* (New York: W.W. Norton & Company, 1985), p. 31.

of the mandate remained uncertain -- not susceptible to immediate analysis. People had voted variously for change and continuity. There had been no referendum on public policy. "Privatization" had not become an economic catch word of the masses. As usual, the plural electorate, comprised of 300 million voters, seem to have been motivated as much, if not more, by parochial regional interests as by national interests. One generalization seems valid: the circumstances and timing of those elections were of critical importance. From this perspective, Rajiv Gandhi's mandate then and now (in 1988) is more qualified and uncertain than the "numbers" would suggest. From this perspective, also, Rajiv Gandhi's personal attributes, his strengths and weaknesses, and his political acumen or lack of it, were less relevant to his reception in India than the nature of his ascension to power. He was invested with an enormous stock of political capital at the outset in a fashion that was independent of his merits and the legacy of his mother. He was perceived as an "outsider" -- someone whose very aloofness from the rough and tumble of politics enhanced his initial worth as a leader.

Rajiv's Potential Shortcomings

Obscured partially in the rush to acclaim him "leader" were Rajiv Gandhi's potential shortcomings. He was not seen as a person who deals with issues within a predictable framework or set of guiding principles. It was said that he lacked a sense of history. If he seemed also to lack a sophisticated vision of India, his advisors and intimates, generally, were not drawn from a cross-section of people who were likely to help him develop the vision he needed to govern successfully over time. In this context, his seeming willingness to rely on his secretariat (augmented at times by old friends and confidants) may have impeded his understanding of complex issues and may have isolated him from political currents in India's disparate regions. This reliance on his secretariat limited the authority of his Cabinet and nullified the emergence of effective leadership in his own Party and in the states. What is more, this reliance on his secretariat reiterated a questionable means of governing India refined by his mother -- and this may be the most damaging part of her legacy, especially if Rajiv Gandhi continues to use the secretariat as a substitute for in-depth understanding of regional issues from the perspectives of regional actors within and outside of the Congress coalition.[5]

Rajiv's Proclaimed Virtues

Rajiv Gandhi's potential shortcomings were partially obscured by the persistent weight of favorable comment about him in India during his first eighteen months as Prime Minister. His virtues were proclaimed, and, in some measure, actually documented by his actions. His initiatives in the Punjab and his approach to an Assam settlement suggested that he was prepared to address complex domestic issues directly, and with a spirit of compromise. People who knew him suggested that he was comfortable with himself, secure in himself, and therefore, unlike Indira Gandhi, prepared to accept compromise on difficult issues rather than to search for means of emerging on top by beating his enemies, real or imagined. It seemed that he actually listened to people and sought accommodation rather than confrontation. He seemed to be the right person in the right place at the right time. He seemed to be capable of giving new direction to India, departing in style and substance from the course set by Mrs. Gandhi. In this context, it was significant that he did not seem to go out of his way to praise his mother publicly or to adhere markedly to policies set in motion by her. He declared, for example, that he never felt that President's Rule (one of Mrs. Gandhi's favorite means of exercising her own and central authority over the states) was an effective policy instrument.

Similarly, at the beginning of his tenure, Rajiv Gandhi demonstrated a capacity to project India's interests in

---

5. It will be difficult for the Prime Minister, whatever his personal inclinations, to break free of reliance on his secretariat in the face of continuing threats on his life. The security apparatus that necessarily strives to protect him also restricts his movement and isolates him.

South Asia without posturing for dramatic effect or repeating some of the cliches concerning "non-alignment" that are time worn and empty of substance. Within the South Asia region, he avoided expounding grand principles of state policy, and often met the leaders of neighboring states in an egalitarian atmosphere that minimized protocol. When, for example, he met with Prime Minister Jayawardene in May of 1985, Gandhi clearly treated the Sri Lankan leader within a framework of respect rooted less in diplomatic formalities than in the regional cultural context in which young people show deference to their elders. The meeting was so successful, according to some sources in Sri Lanka, that India was perceived for the first time in years as being capable of performing a mediating role between the Sinhalese and the Tamils. Rajiv appeared to have achieved a diplomatic success by being simple and direct, rather than haughty and superior (words often used by India's neighbors in South Asia to describe and excoriate India's foreign policy initiatives in the region).

Events following this initial diplomatic success confirm, however, the limitations of style over substance. India's ability to perform a mediating role between the Sinhalese and the Tamils was questioned when India took steps to deport two Tamil militants -- Professor A.S. Balasingham, official spokesman of the Liberation Tigers of Tamil Eelam, and S.C. Chandrahasan, Convenor of the Organization for Protection of Tamils of Eelam from Genocide -- and the Indian-sponsored talks in Bhutan between the Tamils and Prime Minister Jayawardene's principal negotiator broke down. The fact that Balasingham's deportation order was subsequently cancelled did not alter public perceptions that India's mediating role in the Sri Lanka crisis would be difficult and uncertain. While Rajiv Gandhi's initial intervention with Jayawardene had been a grand success, he and India soon had reason to regret involvement in a crisis certain to have persistent, long-term dimensions. It became increasingly apparent that India's role as an intermediary between the Tamils and the Sinhalese was in jeopardy of failure. On December 25, 1985, Steven R. Weisman reported that Indian officials were becoming impatient with the refusal of the "warring parties" to

14

accept a compromise.[6] And, on January 13, 1986, the Press Trust of India reported that the Eelam National Liberation Front, an alliance of Tamil groups, had called off the seven-month-old truce with Sri Lanka's security forces.[7]

The crisis in Sri Lanka continued to deepen, as did India's role in it. The decision of the Government of India in 1987 to airlift supplies, particularly food, to the Tamil population in Jaffna, exacerbated tensions between India and Sri Lanka, and elicited hostile press reaction in many countries, including the United States. The following excerpts from an editorial in *The Washington Post* in June of 1987 are illustrative: "It's not fair what's happening in and to Sri Lanka, the small Indian Ocean democracy ... now fighting for its national life against a secession movement mounted by a terrorist sliver of its 18 percent Tamil minority. The problem is India. ... Ostensibly to provide 'humanitarian relief to Tamil civilians caught up in a Sri Lankan counteroffensive,' the Indian air force last week dropped food and medicine in rebel-held areas. It was a rude intrusion that left some Sri Lankans fearing that a full-scale Indian effort to 'liberate' Tamils could yet come. ... You would think that Prime Minister Rajiv Gandhi, who knows from the Sikhs what it means for a democracy to confront terrorism, would think carefully before offering to civilians relief that is bound to be exploited by terrorists."[8]

While the subsequent decision of the Government of India to send troops to Sri Lanka to "police" a settlement between Tamils and Sinhalese was part of an "accord" signed by Prime Ministers Gandhi and Jayawardene, that decision cannot be assumed to have ended the crisis in Sri Lanka, or India's deep involvement in it. Instead, that decision further emphasizes India's inability to remain

---

6. Weisman, Steven R. "Sri Lanka Strains India's Patience: Resistance by Tamil Guerrillas and Colombo to an Accord has New Delhi Uneasy." *The New York Times*. (December 27, 1985).

7. See "Tamil Guerrilla Groups Call Off Sri Lanka Truce." *The New York Times*. (January 13, 1986).

8. *The Washington Post*. (June 11, 1987), p. A22.

detached from any crisis on its borders perceived to be within its sphere of influence as the dominant power in the South Asia region.

The evolution of Indian policy toward Sri Lanka and recent criticism of that policy illustrate the fact that, however favorable the initial perceptions of Rajiv Gandhi, he has become increasingly vulnerable within India to extreme forms of criticism based on perceptions of his actions. His honeymoon with the Indian media ended within roughly eighteen months of his assumption of the Prime Minister's office. His decline from "grace" has been dramatic and precipitant. Whereas earlier, particularly in 1985, the Prime Minister could do no wrong, and was essentially above criticism, he is in 1988 castigated from all sides, and seems increasingly isolated politically, even within his own party, the Congress (I). India's journalists have exercised their freedom of expression to criticize the Prime Minister in ways that are both acerbic and patronizing: witness the following from the *Economic and Political Weekly* written prior to Mr. Gandhi's disastrous 1987 electoral campaigns in Kerala, West Bengal, and Haryana where his personal involvement in almost frenetic campaigning was insufficient to ensure victory for the Congress (I):

> Adulatory editorial articles are now being gradually replaced by caustic references to the imperial style of functioning. Politicians belonging to opposition groups, who had gone into hibernation, are waking up to the realisation that their profession need not be irretrievably lost. Even within the defunct Congress Party, rumblings of discontent cannot be kept altogether suppressed. The nation, it is being generally acknowledged, is suffering from a deep malaise, and accusatory fingers are being pointed towards just one direction. Lese majeste is suddenly threatening to become passe. ... But why blame the individual? He is merely proving the point that political talent, even political talent of the Machiavellian species, does not necessarily run along hereditary lines; beyond the third or fourth generation, it tends to peter

out. An ordinary young man, totally apolitical, with a limited range of interests in life, fond of rock music and fast cars, has been catapulted into the prime ministerial seat. ... It is not the young man's fault that the so-called power-brokers in the party closed their options and zoomed in upon him. ... It is once more not his fault if sycophants immediately set to work, and elevated him to the status of divinity. A man of rather limited intelligence, he has taken the ingratiating hyperbole addressed to him in season and out of season at its face value. He has convinced himself that he is both omnipotent and omniscient, because, uninterruptedly for months, he has been told so. People have cringed at his feet; as a consequence he has come to consider himself as genuinely cringable. Having been variously provided with intimations of his own immortality, he has come to believe that he is infallible and that the people want him to perform as behoves an absolute monarch." [9]

PERCEPTIONS ROOTED OUTSIDE SOUTH ASIA

Implications of Gandhi's Visit to the Soviet Union

Outside of South Asia, Rajiv Gandhi seems to have created favorable initial images everywhere. This judgment holds, particularly, if assessments of his performance rely for documentation on Indian news accounts of his successes. Some in India, normally sober and circumspect observers of international relations, resorted to hyperbole in recounting Rajiv Gandhi's initial "triumphs of statesmanship." Press accounts (in India) of Rajiv Gandhi's visit to Moscow in May of 1985 were unrestrained in their enthusiasm, almost euphoric in tone.

---

9. "Calcutta Diary" by AM in the *Economic and Political Weekly*, Vol XXII No.9. (February 28, 1987), p. 353.

Beyond what appeared to be an orchestrated chorus of acclaim, there was obvious widespread satisfaction that the new leader had been able to establish his credentials in the Soviet Union. However, in discussing Rajiv Gandhi's performance in the Soviet Union, even independent observers in India tended to gloss over or to ignore the degree to which the Indian Prime Minister may have earned points with his hosts by espousing the Soviet line on critical world issues. The joint communique at the end of the visit could not have been more congenial to Soviet interests had it been drafted by the Soviets alone. And, while the importance of such communiques can be debated, the actual content of this communique (including explicitly negative references to a broad spectrum of U.S. policies -- from the Strategic Defense Initiative to the "invasion" of Grenada) made plain that close Indo-Soviet relations would remain a component of Rajiv Gandhi's foreign policy. Moreover, the timing of the communique (roughly two weeks before the Prime Minister's scheduled visit to the United States) could only reduce expectations in the West (and in the United States in particular) that Rajiv Gandhi's foreign policy would differ markedly from that of Indira Gandhi. The Indian Prime Minister's statements in Russia must have been a disappointment at the time to some observers in the United States who had hoped that Rajiv Gandhi would be more malleable than his mother, and possibly less constrained by ideological blinders. Such expectations focused inordinately on the personality and demeanor of Rajiv Gandhi and gave insufficient attention to long-term Indian perceptions of national interest, including those influenced by United States policies toward Pakistan and China.

Implications of Gandhi's Visit
to the United States

Rajiv Gandhi's visit to the United States in June of 1985 was preceded on the American side by an effort to accept tolerantly the likelihood that India would wish to persist in friendly relations with the Soviet Union, and to build on a parallel basis cordial Indo-American relations. Indian analysis of the visit emphasized that Rajiv Gandhi tried to balance his Soviet and American accounts by emphasizing in his address to the U.S. Congress that India wanted a solution to the crisis in Afghanistan that would ensure the sovereignty, integrity, and non-aligned status of that country. However, though Rajiv Gandhi's statement on Afghanistan was more conciliatory of American interests than earlier Indian pronouncements on that theme, it did not follow that India would press the Soviets to find a political solution to the Afghanistan crisis. While Indian official perceptions of the Afghanistan situation were subsequently, in 1987, probably closer in content to those of the United States, there is no evidence to suggest that India took any initiative diplomatically to encourage the Soviets to initiate their withdrawal from Afghanistan in May of 1988.

Despite some evidence to the contrary, it would appear that neither Indians nor Americans expected much from Rajiv Gandhi's first visit to the United States. Negotiations concerning the primary substantive dimension of the visit were concluded in New Delhi in May of 1985 when Malcolm Baldrige initialled a Memorandum of Understanding (MOU) between the U.S. and India that was said to provide the basis for the liberalization of technology exports from the United States. While this MOU between the two states did subsequently improve the environment for technological transfer from the United States to India, its intent, ultimately, may be diluted by persistent fears in the United States that India will re-export sensitive forms of technology to third countries, including the Soviet Union. In any event, the signing of the MOU was not treated as a major event in India (except possibly by some within India's military establishment who have a persistent interest in acquiring elements of American military technology and in becoming somewhat less dependent on India's principal supplier of such technology, the Soviet Union), possibly because the Indians are already getting, or are likely to get, some of the technology they would like to have from a variety of sources, including Japan.[10] Moreover, the Government of

---

10. In late November of 1985, Rajiv Gandhi visited Japan and signed a technology transfer agreement with the Japanese.

India clearly recognizes that what is not supplied as a derivative of commercial agreements and joint ventures can often be secured by informal means, especially the traffic in ideas that goes on between Indian scientists and technicians on shuttle flights between India and other countries. India is also increasingly capable of improvising its own specialized technology.[11]

It is apparent, in any event, that the prospects for improved Indo-American relations in the Rajiv Gandhi era will be conditioned by United States policies other than those linked to the transfer of technology to India -- notably policies pertaining to Pakistan and China, and Indian perceptions of those policies. For example, the nuclear cooperation agreement signed (in the Summer of 1985) by the United States and China is an obvious obstacle to better relations between India and the United States. The seeming willingness of the United States -- in the context of the Sino-American nuclear agreement -- to accept Chinese verbal assurances that the American technology will be used within China and not re-exported contrasts with the obvious reluctance in some quarters of the Government of the United States to treat India in similar fashion. Even if the United States were to abort or modify the implementation of the Sino-American nuclear cooperation agreement, such action by the United States would not eliminate India's negative perception of the original agreement, especially given India's belief that the Chinese have already been supportive of Pakistan's nuclear weapons program.

Meanwhile, any marginal improvements in Indo-American relations that evolve from the Indo-American Memorandum of Understanding on technology transfer and the subsequent visits of Rajiv Gandhi to the United States can be offset also by other events -- notably, for example, an Indian decision to endorse formally the development of nuclear weapons. Whether or not such a decision has in fact been made by

---

11. For example, unable to purchase an Airborne Warning and Control System, AWACS, from Western sources, India began the development of its own AWACS to be installed on British Hawker Siddeley 748 airliners being manufactured by Hindustan Aeronautics.

India, it has been increasingly evident in the 1980s that Indian intellectuals, retired military officers, and others linked to the political establishment have been pressing for a full fledged Indian nuclear weapons program. Segments of the Indian press, notably the *Times of India*, have also lent support to those in India who seem committed to nuclear weapons development. It is noteworthy that the proponents of nuclear weapons in India are some of the same people who are deeply committed to new technology in general. They want India to establish its credentials as a first-rate power -- a nation to be reckoned with not only in South Asia, but also beyond that region of India's obvious dominance. They are spurred on less by developments in Pakistan than by nationalistic zeal and the belief that having nuclear weapons not only is an ultimate symbol of scientific advancement and national power, but also is a means of gaining international credibility as a world power. There is little hard evidence to suggest that there has been a decisive shift toward a nuclear weapons policy in India. Rajiv Gandhi has repeatedly suggested that there is no such shift, and has spoken in favor of nuclear disarmament.[12] Whatever happens in this sphere, it seems obvious that American perceptions of India would be affected adversely, at least in the short-run, if the Government of India did decide to endorse formally a nuclear weapons development program -- especially in the light of United States concern about the proliferation of nuclear weapons and India's evident reluctance to support U.S. non-proliferation undertakings. Of course, it must be recognized in this context that the policy of the United States concerning non-proliferation is not a model of consistency. While the U.S.S.R. has been in Afghanistan, the United States has been exceedingly reluctant to chastise Pakistan for its evident attempt to acquire nuclear weapons.

---

12. See, for example, Prime Minister Gandhi's June 9, 1988, address to the third special session on disarmament of the United Nations General Assembly, as printed in the June, 1988 edition of *India News* (a monthly publication of the Embassy of India, 2107 Massachusetts Avenue, N.W. Washington, D.C.).

THE LEADER'S ROLE IN CONTEMPORARY INDIA

It has become fashionable both within and outside of India, especially among political scientists, to speculate on the changes of style and substance that would be effected if the current Prime Minister ceased to hold office following the next General Elections (which could be scheduled for the Spring of 1989). Such speculation has become a cliche-ridden game -- a game played periodically in India without reference generally to real people. Yet, the ground rules for the game are well-established within the framework of conventional wisdom. We all know in advance that the new leader must embody in the abstract whole sets of contradictions. He (or she) must hail from the Hindi-speaking belt of northern states, be untainted by the presumed prejudices of any given region, and have the personal appeal of an "all-India politician." While speaking fluent Hindi, he must be deferential to the linguistic and other traditions of the South, and at the same time sensitive to the history, culture and literary traditions of Bengal. He must be supportive of linguistic states, but hostile to certain expressions of linguistic nationalism. He must be committed to social and economic change, but not so committed to such change that he fails to see value in maintaining institutions of tradition. He must be strong and charismatic, yet capable of using the language of compromise and the idiom of "saintly" politics. He must mobilize votes with ruthless skill, exploiting when necessary India's linguistic and communal divisions, and, at the same time, must defend citizens' rights without regard to language, caste, class or religion. The ideal leader of India must have all of these attributes and, if possible of course, hail from the most populous state, Uttar Pradesh!

Perhaps the best means of challenging such persistent popular perceptions of the needed characteristics in an all-India leader is to suggest, as I do now, that one of India's most promising leaders was Prime Minister Lal Bahadur Shastri -- a man who did not fit the hypothetical model of an ideal leader, even though he was a Hindi-speaking Uttar Pradeshi! Indeed, when he succeeded India's first Prime Minister, Jawaharlal Nehru, Shastri did not seem at the outset to have many of the attributes so frequently assumed to be necessary in governing India.

"Here was no dashing young man on a white charger, as a ton of legend and a few ounces of fact had made Nehru in the public mind before he became Prime Minister; nor was he, as Nehru was, an innovator of ideas. On the contrary, here was an embarrassingly plain Prime Minister, humble to a fault, so innocent of the outward signs of the Leader that no one thought he would have the thrust to break out of the prevailing gloom."[13] There was no single attribute of Lal Bahadur Shastri that fitted the stereotype of the all-India leader. He was small of stature (five feet two inches), and almost doll-like in appearance. His voice was soft, not easily projected without a microphone. His manner was so deferential to the views of others that he seemed to lack convictions of his own. He was not drawn from the urban, educated elite. He was a villager. He had been educated in India at Kashi Vidyapeeth, rather than at an institution overseas. Indeed, he had never travelled outside of India until he became Prime Minister. "It was once said of Shastri that he was a humble man with much to be humble about. The witticism was misleading. Whatever Shastri achieved, he owed entirely to himself. He had no rich father to support him; his father, a modest teacher, died when he was a year and a half old. No patron crowned him his successor."[14] Yet Shastri, in his short tenure in office confirmed by his demeanor in war and in peace that he was unusually capable of performing his constitutional functions within the framework of India's plural society. It is my view that India has a veritable "reserve army" of such men and women, and therefore can dare to focus as a people on persistent issues of political economy -- questions that are more interesting and important than "Who will resolve our problems for us and lead us into the future?"

---

13. Chopra, Pran. *Uncertain India*. (London: Asia Publishing House, 1968), p. 283.

14. Zinkin, Taya. *Challenges in India*. (London: Chatts and Windus, 1966), p. 27.

2

THE ARENA OF
CENTRE-STATE RELATIONS

THE NEED FOR ISSUE ORIENTATION

Analysis of more than three years of the "Rajiv Gandhi Era" has given us some sense of his personal attributes and his style of governing. It is evident, however, that analysis of Gandhi's personal style, his habits of mind, and his policy preferences will not provide, by itself, an understanding of the manner in which he will govern in the future, the action decisions his government will make, or the policies his nation will follow. Persistent issues in India have constrained Rajiv Gandhi's options and shaped the nature of his regime. And, while political pundits will continue to speculate about what Prime Minister Gandhi might do if he had the freedom to follow his own instincts, it has become increasingly important to understand and anticipate the pressures that will determine his actions (or those of any Prime Minister) by limiting his freedom of choice.

While it cannot be argued that the leader and his coterie are irrelevant to analysis of issues and perceived trends in India, the emphasis in this essay is on the environment in which the leader, and those around him, must function. This places the leader in a context where his personal attributes, real or imagined, are less important than the pressures that constrain him. The approach consciously "devalues" the leader and his role by emphasizing that he is not free to act in a fashion that is independent of variables of much larger significance than his personal preferences.

Identification of the persistent issues and problems of contemporary India that constitute the context in which a leader must govern will help us to establish a more reliable, long-term means of predicting the policy choices of the Government of India. The trick, of course, is to discern the issues that matter and that are likely to be "persistent" over time. Because there is no scientific means of determining in advance which contemporary issues will be persistent, normative judgments are inevitable. The issue for the social scientist is not to pretend to eschew normative judgments, but to make certain that readers understand clearly when such judgments have been made. Because I do not believe that social science can be either omniscient or perfectly objective, I have endeavored in the Preface to this work to expose aspects of my background, experience and training, that condition my perspectives on the themes I am articulating. With this qualification, I have selected three arenas in contemporary India within which there will be persistent issues that will shape the agenda for those who govern India in the years ahead:[1]

    a) the arena of Centre-state relations;
    b) the arena of the national economy; and
    c) the arena of national security.

THE POLITICS OF ACCOMMODATION AND CONFRONTATION

With regard to the arena of Centre-state relations in India, there is ample evidence to suggest that the members of India's Constituent Assembly (India's Founding Fathers) met to create a "minimal federation," but ended up creating what Granville Austin has called "a new kind of

---

1. My "time frame" concerning what I am calling persistent issues "in the years ahead" is intentionally non-specific. I am not a "futurist". Neither am I claiming here to predict the long-term prospects of India. If pressed, I would say only that I am trying, utilizing my knowledge and experience in India since 1956, to make informed judgments and educated guesses about issues that are likely to be persistent over the next ten to fifteen years, leading into the 21st Century.

federalism,"[2] evolved out of the perceived threats to the unity of India and driven by the then recent experience of the partition, as well as other events, including the military confrontation with Pakistan in Kashmir and the rural-based insurrection in Telengana in South India. In effect, *The Constitution of India* was conceived in an atmosphere of fear of the breakup of the newly independent nation into autonomous or semi-autonomous states. It's provisions, therefore, consciously tilted in the direction of a strong Centre, fully capable of encroaching on the powers of the states. At the same time, the Constitution accorded sufficient explicit and residual powers to the states to ensure a constant tension between the central government and the states as each, in time, would seek to interpret and enlarge on constitutional prerogatives.[3]

The dynamic tension between the Centre and the states was neither obvious nor pronounced as long as one political party, the Congress, was dominant throughout the Indian subcontinent. When the Congress ruled at the Centre and in most of the states, and when India's first Prime Minister, Jawaharlal Nehru, was at the zenith of his power, areas of potential discord between the Centre and the states were not permitted to become sources of deep division and unresolved tension. It has been said that the "politics of accommodation" prevailed in the first decade of India's independence.[4] The atmosphere was such that even an issue of extremely divisive potential, the pressure to transform the map of India by creating new territorial divisions based on language, could be addressed and acted

---

2. Austin, Granville. *The Indian Constitution: Cornerstone of a Nation.* (Oxford: Clarendon Press, 1966), p. 193.

3. The Seventh Schedule of the Constitution attempted to rationalize and specify the division of authority between the Centre and the states; it included a Union list of functions, a state list and a concurrent list. However, nothing in the Seventh Schedule would end the ambiguities resulting from overlapping functions in the lists.

4. In this context, see, for example, Kothari, Rajni. *Politics in India.* (Boston: Little, Brown and Company, 1970), pp. 109-116.

upon, even though Nehru had misgivings about the creation
of "linguistic states."[5]   After Nehru's death and following
the breakup of the Congress' monolithic control of the
country in 1967, tensions between the central government
and the states were less amenable to resolution, especially
when Prime Minister Indira Gandhi's style of governance
was confrontational, rather than accommodating of states'
interests.   If Nehru opted to secure the unity of India by
accepting the plural nature of the country and endorsing
diversity, Mrs. Gandhi sought the same end by radically
different means.   She would preserve the unity of India,
not by accommodating the regional interests of a plural
society, but by concentrating power in her own hands at
the Centre and by rooting out and destroying politically
those who seemed to challenge her authority.   In this
process she would employ every instrument of power at her
disposal, including the Army, to impress her will and to
confirm her authority.

Ultimately, Mrs. Gandhi's final acts were played out in
the arena of Centre-state relations, and the old question of
linguistic states would be a residual issue having bearing
on events in the Punjab, including the final confrontation
between the central government, using the Army, and the
dissident Sikhs barricaded in the Golden Temple at
Amritsar.

THE CRISIS IN THE PUNJAB

The Centre-state dimensions of the crisis in the Punjab
have deep roots which can best be understood in historical

---

5. Though he is said to have opposed linguistic states in principle, believing
that such states would promote "linguistic nationalism" and weaken the fragile
basis of unity in the country, Nehru acquiesced in their creation in order to
remove a major source of discord.   His motivation seems clear, but the
question persists as to whether the decision to permit states' reorganization
along linguistic lines in 1956 avoided discord or, in fact, perpetuated it —
legitimizing in perpetuity the claims of linguistic (and other) minorities to
states of their own.

context.[6] It should be remembered that the Indian Punjab has been partitioned twice in the last forty years: once in 1947 and, again, in 1966. From the perspective of Sikhs, the 1947 division "gave" Pakistan more than 80 percent of the richest and best irrigated land formerly included in the undivided Punjab.[7]

For many years following 1947, the Sikhs sought to have a dominant voice in a state of their own within the boundaries of India. Indeed, they petitioned for a Punjabi-speaking state in the 1950s and were chagrined when the Nehru-appointed States Reorganization Commission acceded to the linguistic reorganization of the map of India but rejected the Sikh's linguistic argument for the Punjab. The issue was complicated by the fact that the Sikh claim made plain that the written language of a new linguistic state would be Punjabi in the *Gurmukhi* script. While there could be no question that the oral language of the Punjab was Punjabi (the vernacular of all communities, Sikh, Hindu and Moslem, prior to partition), the specification of the *Gurmukhi* script (a script devised by the Sikh's second Guru for the Sikh scriptures) contributed to the perception that the Sikhs were in fact seeking to establish a theocratic, rather than a linguistic, state. For some, including Jawaharlal Nehru, this made the Sikhs' demand communal, rather than linguistic. Many Punjabi-speaking Hindus shared Nehru's skepticism and began (as confirmed in the 1961 census) to record their language as Hindi in implicit rejection of a Punjabi state in which their interests might be subordinated to those of the Sikhs.

Ironically, it was Mrs. Gandhi in 1966 who agreed to the formation of a Punjabi-speaking state. (Her decision may have been motivated, at least in part, by the performance of Sikhs, civilian and military alike, in the 1965 war with Pakistan.) However, in the process, the

---

6. For extended discussion of the Punjab crisis, see two recent books: *Amritsar: Mrs. Gandhi's Last Battle* by Mark Tully and Satish Jacob, and *What's Happening to India?* by Robin Jeffrey.

7. Nayer, Baldev Raj. *Minority Politics in the Punjab.* (Princeton: Princeton University Press, 1966), p. 293.

erstwhile Punjab was divided into three states: Haryana, Himachel Pradesh and the residual state of Punjab. The "residual" Punjab, now a "Sikh-majority state," had to share a common capital, Chandigarh, with the new state of Haryana. Also important from the perspective of many Sikhs was the fact that the new boundary between Haryana and the Punjab (established by the 1966 partition and drawn only roughly to meet a linguistic criterion) placed some Punjabi-speaking areas in Hindi-speaking Haryana, thereby diminishing by that number the majority of Punjabi-speakers in the Punjab. In addition, the new boundary left the Sikhs in the Punjab with a Sikh majority of only 56 percent, insufficient (because the Sikhs could not be expected to vote in a single bloc) to ensure a dominant voice for the Sikhs in the state. It was thereby assured that the dominant party of the Sikhs (the Akali Dal) would have difficulty governing in the new Punjab except in alliance with Hindu parties. The Sikhs had achieved a Pyrrhic victory. The stage was now set for new Sikh demands -- demands that would eventually prove to be unacceptable to Mrs. Gandhi and the central government of India, that would result in violent confrontation between the contending forces, and that would lead, finally, to Mrs. Gandhi's death by assassination.

Relations between New Delhi (the Centre) and the Punjab became increasingly difficult in the 1970s. Tensions grew as Mrs. Gandhi sought increasingly to exercise central authority over the Punjab and other Indian states. In a sense, this dimension of the Punjab crisis is rooted in different interpretations of the Indian Constitution. While the Constitution (under Article 246) attempts to establish a division of responsibility and authority between the "Union" (i.e., the central government) and the states, there has been a persistent tug-of-war over the actual division of authority in day-to-day operations of government. In practice, this has meant that the central government characteristically has had the capacity to proclaim and to initiate programs, in the field of rural economic development for example, while the states could vitiate the implementation of such programs.[8]   Such a division of authority between the Centre and the states would frustrate any activist Prime Minister of the Republic.   It is not surprising that Indira Gandhi, given her insecurities and apparent need for power, increasingly sought more absolute means during her tenure in office of exercising central control over the states, if necessary by exploiting the emergency powers of the Constitution under "President's Rule."

In the case of the Punjab, Mrs. Gandhi's propensity to use President's Rule was increased when, following her defeat in the General Elections of 1977 and the period of Janata rule, she returned to power in the parliamentary elections of January, 1980.   She found the Punjab's government in the hands of a Janata coalition (comprised essentially of the Akali Dal in alliance with the Jan Sangh).   She proceeded to use President's Rule[9] to dissolve the state's legislative assembly and to require new elections -- leading to the election of persons favored by her.

---

8. In this context, it is noteworthy that it is the states of India, rather than the central government in New Delhi, that have authority over agricultural development.   This means, in practice, that the central government has no constitutional authority to levy an agricultural income tax or to ensure that a particular concept of agrarian reform is instituted uniformly in the states.

9. Mrs. Gandhi, at the same time, declared President's Rule in seven additional states where her authority was being challenged by persons and parties opposed to her.   In essence, the "President's Rule" clauses of *The Constitution of India* (Articles 356 and 357) permit the President of India, i.e., the central government, to "... assume all or any of the functions of the Government of a State;" to "... declare that the powers of the Legislature of the State shall be exercisable by or under the authority of Parliament;" and even to suspend "... in whole or in part the operation of any provisions of this Constitution relating to any body or authority in the State."   It is widely perceived in India that Article 356 has been used capriciously by the central government on many occasions.   Article 356 is an anathema to political parties in opposition to the Congress (I).   [See, for example, the "White Paper" by the Government of Karnataka, in *Centre-State Relations*, edited by Sati Sahni, and published in Delhi by Vikas Publishing House Pvt. Ltd., 1984, pages 260-291.]

Following the assassination of Indira Gandhi on October 31, 1984, and the subsequent riots of reaction that led to the killing of hundreds of Sikhs in New Delhi,[10] the Punjab has drawn more than its share of headlines. Both the indigenous news media and foreign media have publicized events related to the Punjab:

-- the "terrorist" bombings in Delhi and New Delhi in May of 1985,

---

10. It is common knowledge that a number of politicians linked to the Congress (I) either arranged or gave tacit support for the "counter-violence" against Sikhs, especially in Delhi, that followed Indira Gandhi's death. In this context, it is useful to review the "Report of a Joint Inquiry into the Causes and Impact of the Riots in Delhi from 31 October to 10 November"; this citizens' report, *Who are the Guilty?*, was put together by respected persons of the People's Union for Democratic Rights (President, Gobinda Mukhoty), and the People's Union for Civil Liberties (President, Rajni Kothari). The report was published in November, 1984, by Mukhoty and Kothari and printed at Sunny Graphica, Rohtas Nagar, Shahadara, Delhi - 110 054. Because the February, 1987, report of a government commission, headed by Ranganath Misra, rejected allegations that the Delhi riots were organized by the Congress (I) and explicitly exonerated H.K.L. Bhagat, a Congress leader named in literally hundreds of affidavits as being one of the leaders of the violence, it has been widely perceived in India to be unsatisfactory, and possibly a calculated means of minimizing further damage to the reputation of the ruling Congress Party. For this reason, the Mukhoty-Kothari report assumes additional importance three and one-half years after the events. Meanwhile, the Government's apparent inability, or unwillingness, to bring charges against persons involved in the killing of Sikhs following Mrs. Gandhi's assassination has become a pregnant political issue among Sikhs in India and elsewhere. In these circumstances, Prime Minister Rajiv Gandhi has been unable, even, to put distance between himself and some of those persons in the Congress (I) who were named in the Mukhoty-Kothari report as having been directly or indirectly involved in the "orchestrated" violence against the Sikhs. This clearly adds to his own political vulnerability on the issue. And, it must be assumed that Rajiv Gandhi remains a target on extremist "hit" lists. There is no reason to believe that there is a "statute of limitations" on Sikh anger at the magnitude of arson, lynching and burning alive visited upon their community in Delhi and its suburbs following Mrs. Gandhi's assassination.

-- the almost immediate passage without debate of *The Terrorist and Disruptive Activities (Prevention) Act* by the Indian Parliament,[11]
-- Rajiv Gandhi's dramatic negotiations with Harchand Singh Longowal in July of 1985,
-- Longowal's subsequent assassination by dissident Sikhs,
-- the elections in September, 1985, that produced a victory for the Akali Dal over Rajiv's Congress,[12]
-- the failure of the Centre to implement the 1985 Gandhi-Longowal accord,
-- the persistence of extremist agitation and killing in the Punjab,
-- and Delhi's dismissal of the Akali government and imposition of rule by the Centre ("President's rule") in 1987.

Complementing the headlines have been reports suggesting that the crisis in the Punjab derived from religious extremists who threatened the unity of India by agitating for secession from the Republic. While one cannot ignore the fact that the Akali Dal[13] has been

---

11. The almost hysterical climate in New Delhi following the bombings of May 10-12, 1985, is reflected in the provisions of this Act -- an Act submitted by the ruling party and passed without discussion by the Parliament. The Act, if strictly enforced, would sharply limit individual freedom in India, making it possible for the state to prosecute, for example, a cartoonist whose drawings might be perceived as contributing to tensions and violence between or among groups.

12. From the perspective of those looking for ways of defusing tensions between the Punjab and the Centre, the Congress's electoral losses in 1985 conferred transitory "disguised gains," especially when Rajiv Gandhi accepted defeat gracefully by declaring that India had won by demonstrating capacity (albeit with an unparalleled mobilization of armed men to keep the peace during the voting) to carry out successful democratic elections in the face of intimidation.

13. Akali Dal means literally "army of the faithful." Now a full-fledged political party, the Akali Dal owes its origins to a movement in the 1920s to

(continued...)

32

associated historically with plans dating from the early days of World War II for *Azad Punjab* (free Punjab) and, later, for *Sikhistan* or *Khalistan* (land of the chosen), it is misleading to interpret the contemporary crisis in the Punjab in terms that separate it either from a persistent crisis (not limited to the Punjab) in the division of authority between the Centre and the states, or from a variety of other issues, including ones stemming indirectly from successful rural development policies associated with the "Green Revolution" in India.

The crisis in the Punjab in the 1980s is rooted in the 1947 and 1966 "partitions" and the constant searching of Sikhs for a homeland in which they could be dominant. It is rooted in the persistent struggle for authority between those who rule at the Centre and those who occupy power in the states. It is rooted in the style of governance of Indira Gandhi. It is also associated, paradoxically, with the Punjab's spectacular economic success over the last two decades (roughly from the mid-sixties to the present).[14] That success can be attributed to the process

---

13(...continued)
effect reform in the management and operation of Sikh temples or *gurudwaras*. The success of this movement produced two institutions that have been prominent in the life of the Punjab ever since: the Shiromani Gurdwara Prabandhak Committee and the Akali Dal. The former institution, known popularly as the SGPC, began as a "management committee" for the Golden Temple, and later acquired effective control over *gurudwaras* in the Punjab, Haryana, Himachel Pradesh, and Chandigarh, together with their incomes. "The funds available to the SGPC, as well as its influence over religious life, made it a magnet for ambitious Sikh politicians. In the Sikh majority Punjab formed in 1966, the SGPC became an organization which could create and destroy governments." [Jeffrey, Robin. *What's Happening to India?*, p. 66.] The latter institution, the Akali Dal, began as a unit fighting for the causes of the SGPC. The Akali Dal later became the dominant political party among Sikhs, especially among Sikh Jats, the industrious peasant farmers of the Punjab.

14. The economic success and political turmoil in the Punjab are inextricably linked to rapidly rising expectations among the people -- expectations that would generate pressure on any government, whatever its capacities and

(continued...)

by which sturdy, self-reliant Jat farmers (acclaimed appropriately by a British authority on the Punjab, the late Sir Malcolm Darling, as "the best cultivators in India")[15] used high yielding varieties of seed, together with fertilizer and appropriate and timely amounts of water, and produced sustained increases in agricultural production -- ensuring that the Punjab of the 1970s would become India's breadbasket and the most prosperous state in the Republic.[16] "Between 1964-1965 and 1977-1978, Punjab trebled its output of food-grains - from 3.4 million tonnes to 10.3 million tonnes. Punjab stands out as the state which has most successfully introduced the new agricultural

---

14(...continued)

willingness to respond to pressure. The entire phenomenon reminds me of a prescient statement of Sir Malcolm Darling, who spent the greater part of his life working for the economic development of the Punjab. Said Darling, "Below a certain standard of living men tend to be inarticulate, but once they rise above this point they not only feel but assert their grievances." [Darling, Sir Malcolm. *The Punjab Peasant in Prosperity and Debt*. 3rd edition. (London: Oxford University Press, 1932), pp. 132-133.]

15. Darling, Sir Malcolm. *The Punjab Peasant in Prosperity and Debt*. pp. 34-36.

16. There is a tendency for some, especially Americans, to believe that the agricultural success story in the Punjab can be attributed mainly to "new technology in agriculture" (particularly high yielding varieties of wheat), introduced in the Punjab in the late 1960s by the Government of India through the "good offices" of the Rockefeller and Ford Foundations, together with the United States Agency for International Development (USAID). While the contributions of these American institutions should not, in my view, be seen as incidental to the subsequent increases in agricultural production, the successful achievements in the Punjab owe much also to prior investments in irrigation, to the prior development of institutions providing rural credit, to the quality of the Jat farmers, and to the fortuitous existence in the region of a land system in which (unlike many regions of India) those enjoying secure rights in land also tended to be the tillers of the soil -- a land system that was conducive to economic progress. If the new technology alone were the critical input, as some would have it, then India's poorest state, Bihar, with better quality land than the Punjab and a high water table in its agricultural zones, might have been expected easily by 1988 to have emulated the Punjab.

techniques. More than 90 percent of its area under wheat,
and more than 85 per cent under rice, are planted with
high yielding varieties."[17]

However, agricultural success in the Punjab was not
without its dark side: the financial returns from what
became known popularly (and somewhat misleadingly) as the
Green Revolution were "... primarily confined to the
already prosperous Punjabi farmers."[18] Widening income
inequality was a concomitant feature of the success story.
And, while the Green Revolution did not cause "poverty" in
the Punjab, those who were not full participants in
economic progress (notably small farmers and landless
peasants) were placed in a position of at least "relative
deprivation" -- as they perceived it.[19] And, according to
some observers, political extremism, nurtured by Sant
Jarnail Singh Bhindranwale,[20] drew support in the early

---

17. Jeffrey, Robin. *What's Happening to India?* p. 29.

18. Bryjak, George J. "The Economics of Assassination: The Punjab Crisis
and the Death of Indira Gandhi." *Asian Affairs - An American Review.*
(Washington, D.C.: Heidret Publications, Spring, 1985), p. 29.

19. The Green Revolution in the Punjab has obviously benefitted most
directly the twenty-three percent of families who own two-thirds of the
land. Meanwhile, approximately one-third of rural Punjabis are landless.
The landless increasingly must compete for jobs with migrant laborers from
the poorest sections of the peasantry of eastern Uttar Pradesh, Bihar, and
elsewhere. The fact that many of the migrant laborers, who are Hindu, seem
to be staying-on in the Punjab threatens also to reduce the proportion of
Sikhs in the State, and can be used, in any event, by Sikh fundamentalists to
prey on traditional fears that "Hinduism" might drown the Sikh's identity as a
separate community. After all, Sikhs are a tiny minority of "Indians"; they
comprise no more than 12 million of the people of India, less than two
percent of the total population.

20. There are various explanations circulated for the emergence of
Bhindranwale himself. Murray J. Leaf has cited a draft paper by Paul
Wallace (entitled "The Dilemma of Sikh Revivalism") to suggest that
Bhindranwale was supported financially during the Janata period by Indira
Gandhi's son, Sanjay Gandhi, and by Zail Singh, later the President of India,

(continued...)

1980s mainly from sections of the rural poor who had indeed been bypassed by the Green Revolution and whose interests did not coincide with the landowning Sikh Jats who have dominated the leadership of the Akali Dal.[21]

The continuing crisis in the Punjab has other dimensions, as well. As noted earlier, these dimensions are clearly subsumed within the context of Centre-state relations in which the states feel deprived of status and vulnerable to the decisions of a "ruling elite" in the central government. The issues of contention are often less significant than the symbolism that grows up around them. Consider the persistent dispute over the city of Chandigarh. Having "lost" Lahore in the first partition of the Punjab in 1947, and having been denied the second city of the Punjab, Amritsar, as capital of the new Indian state because of Amritsar's nearness to the border with Pakistan, the Sikhs and other Punjabis were made the beneficiaries

---

20(...continued)
as a means of widening differences with the Akali Dal and to "... break up the political cooperation between Akali Dal and the urban and Hindu-oriented Jan Sangh which was the heart of the Janata in Punjab." [Leaf, Murray J. "The Punjab in Crisis." *Asian Survey* Vol. XXV, No.5, (May 1985), pp. 475-498. For additional speculation and fact on the links between the Congress (I) and the rise of Sant Jarnail Singh Bhindranwale, see Chapter 4 of *Amritsar: Mrs. Gandhi's Last Battle* by Mark Tully and Satish Jacob.]

21. It is said that some early disciples of Bhindranwale were Naxalites, left wing extremists committed to violent revolution. Mark Tully and Satish Jacob, citing an "official" briefing in April 1984, have reported that the number of hardcore followers of Bhindranwale were then considered by the Government of India to be between 400 and 500, a quarter of whom were thought to be students (from the All India Sikh Students Federation) and the rest Naxalites. [Tully and Jacob. *Amritsar*, p. 124.] How many of these might be classified roughly as coming from the "rural poor" remains in question. Astute observers of the situation in the Punjab, e.g., Surjit Mansingh, have told me that many of the dissidents were, in fact, drawn from the idle sons of the well-to-do. Whatever the basis of the recruitment of those who initially followed Bhindranwale, the context of his martyrdom at the Golden Temple in June of 1984 and the anti-Sikh riots in Delhi in October-November, 1984, have contributed to a sense of alienation from the central government among even the most moderate Sikhs from every stratum of the community.

of an entirely new city, Chandigarh. Chandigarh was built
with central government support and was designed by the
illustrious French architect, Le Corbusier. While the city
is, from my perspective, an architectural disaster,[22] it has
itself become a bone of contention between the Punjab and
Haryana -- following the second partition of the Punjab in
1966. Instead of awarding Chandigarh to the Punjab, the
"interim solution" at the time was to have the city
administered by the central government and to have its
secretariat divided in its functions between the Punjab and
Haryana. Later, in a move to appease the Sikhs, Mrs.
Gandhi actually promised that Chandigarh would go to the
Punjab. But the award was never implemented. Ironically,
Rajiv Gandhi also promised to resolve the Chandigarh issue
during his negotiations with Harchand Singh Longowal in
July of 1985 concerning Sikh grievances. Once again, it
was announced that Chandigarh would be transferred to the
Punjab. Indeed, it was specified initially that the transfer
would take place on Republic Day, January 26, 1986.
However, the transfer was not effected then nor has it
taken place as of June of 1988. Instead, it was delayed
indefinitely when the Prime Minister's own Party in
Haryana argued that it would lose power if Chandigarh was
conceded to the Punjab, and if the remaining provisions of
the Longowal accord were implemented. The Centre was in
a "no win" situation: not to implement the accord would
add to the sense of alienation of Sikhs, including
moderates in no way associated with the demand for an
independent Khalistan, yet to implement it would threaten
the Congress's own political base in Haryana. In the end,
the Centre discounted the political costs in the Punjab,

---

22. While the government complex at Chandigarh is widely acclaimed by Le
Corbusier's admirers, the dominant theme of the city in its structural outline
is "compartmentation". In a plural society already divided hierarchically by
income and caste, but seeking officially to establish a more egalitarian,
secular, democratic social system, what could be more anomalous than the
creation of an entirely new city divided into "sectors" (virtually walled
ghettoes in their original design) so disposed geographically that the affluent,
including ministers and officials of government, could walk from their homes
to the secretariat, while the lower ranks, living in their own distant sectors,
would have to travel by bus, bicycle, or on foot to get to work?

where the Congress (I) had already lost to the Akali Dal in
September of 1985, and sought to retain the Congress (I)
base in Haryana by appeasing its own Party's stalwarts,
including the Chief Minister, Bhajan Lal.   The Longowal
accord was not implemented.   The Centre tilted toward
Haryana, but Rajiv Gandhi and the Congress (I) nonetheless
lost the subsequent state election in Haryana on June 17,
1987.   More than 20 years of wrangling over the future of
Chandigarh had produced little more than frustration and
alienation on all sides.

Another bone of contention between the Punjab and
New Delhi has to do with the pace of industrialization in
the State.   The tangible economic success in the Punjab
has been based obviously on progress in agriculture, rather
than industry.   As Robin Jeffrey has observed, "Less than
25 per cent of Punjab's gross domestic product comes from
industry, a share which is one of the lowest in India, even
below states like Kerala (30 per cent), Madhya Pradesh (31
per cent) or Bihar (31 per cent), though the per capita
GDP of these states is far behind that of the Punjab."[23]
While it is also clear that the Punjab's agricultural
performance is such that it actually acts to reduce the
percentage share of industry in its Gross Domestic Product,
evidence is frequently marshalled in the Punjab to suggest
that the central government has designed its investment in
modern industry so as to discriminate against the Punjab in
the allocation of major projects -- particularly prestigious
projects in large and medium industries.   While such a
charge of central government discrimination in the
allocation of industrial projects cannot easily be confirmed,
it is evident that the government's own data can be used
crudely to add credibility to the charge.   For example, the
Seventh Plan's proposed expenditures for large and medium
industrial projects would place the Punjab tenth among
states of the Union -- after Uttar Pradesh, Maharashtra,
West Bengal, Andhra Pradesh, Tamil Nadu, Kerala, Gujarat
and Bihar (with the rank order based on the magnitude of
proposed industrial expenditure by the Government of India

---

23. Jeffrey, Robin. *What's Happening to India?* p. 34.

in those states during the Seventh Plan period, 1985-90).[24]
On the other hand, as the tension mounted between New
Delhi and the dissidents in the Spring of 1984, and as Mrs.
Gandhi made the fateful decision to send the army into the
Golden Temple at Amritsar to crush Bhindranwale and his
followers, industrial output was growing in the Punjab at a
rate double the national average. [25]

While the failure of the central government to locate
more public sector industry in the Punjab is sometimes
attributed to official reluctance to place strategic
industries in a border state susceptible to attack or
"destabilization" by Pakistan, there seems no escaping the
baseline fact that states like Uttar Pradesh, historically the
Congress (I) bastion in the Hindi-speaking heartland of the
north because of its size and the number of persons it
sends to Parliament, will always have much more clout in
securing resources from the Centre than the Punjab, even
if the Punjab were controlled by a government disposed to
work amicably with the Centre.

Finally, the almost intractable nature of the
Centre-state crisis in the Punjab is made plain by the
content and tone of the 1973 resolution (the Anandpur
Sahib Resolution)[26] drawn up by the Working Committee of

---

24. *The Seventh Five Year Plan, 1985-90.* Volume II. (New Delhi:
Government of India, The Planning Commission, October 1985), p. 200.

25. Tully and Jacob. *Amritsar.* p. 48.

26. There have been several "versions" of what is called the Anandpur Sahib
Resolution. According to Robin Jeffrey, "The version deemed authentic by
the president of the Akali Dal, Sant Harchand Singh Longowal, in 1982,
spoke of guarding and propagating the Sikh faith. It called for the addition to
Punjab of various pieces of neighboring states and for greatly increased
autonomy from the central government, not just for Punjab but for all the
Indian states. .... It was a confused and confusing document, hinting at
semi-autonomy in places and stressing in others the need to look after Sikhs
in the army and other central-government services." For the Centre, the least
acceptable features of the Anandpur Sahib Resolution are those that would
alter the constitutionally established terms of reference concerning the
division of authority between the central government and the states. [See
Robin Jeffrey's *What's Happening to India?* pp. 128-129.]

the Akali Dal to articulate the aims and objectives of the Sikh community.[27] The resolution raised some demands for regional autonomy that, from the perspective of any central government of India, are likely to be non-negotiable: namely, that the central government's "interference" in the affairs of the state be limited to Defence, Foreign Relations, Currency, and General Communications. The resolution also expressed concern about a new recruitment policy for the army that, if implemented vigorously, would have restricted the Sikhs' share of new recruits to little more than 2 per cent (a number based on the Sikhs' share of the national population), and eroded the Sikhs' sense of pride and identity with their military tradition. And, the resolution raised economic issues equally laden with emotion. Among these was the Sikh farmers' proprietary concern about water rights, and their fear, whether rational or not, that the central government's proposed sharing of the "Punjab's water" with the people of the neighboring states of Haryana and Rajasthan would lead to water shortages in the Punjab. From the perspective of many Sikhs, the demands articulated in the Anandpur Sahib Resolution have never been dealt with by the central government. With the passage of time the resolution has become a symbol of unresolved issues that exacerbate tensions between the Centre and those who claim to speak for the Sikh community.

Thus, in 1988, the demands of the Anandpur Sahib Resolution, whether representative of the Sikh community as a whole or not, remain "on the table" -- to be addressed meaningfully or dismissed by the Centre. That is to say, almost three years after the Longowal accord was announced by Rajiv Gandhi to cheering members of Parliament and hailed as the vehicle through which the crisis in the Punjab would be resolved, the relationship

---

27. There is a certain presumptuousness in the Akali Dal's claim to articulate the goals of the Sikh community as a whole. Mark Tully and Satish Jacob have rightly observed that, while the Akali Dal, in the framework of its Anandpur Sahib Resolution, purports to speak for all Sikhs, "In no election so far has the Akali Dal got 50 per cent of the total Sikh vote. In fact only one section of the Sikh community has consistently supported the Akali Dal -- the Jat caste of peasant farmers." [Tully and Jacob. *Amritsar.* p. 47.]

between the Centre and the Punjab remains strained. The initial euphoria generated by the "accord" has long since been dissipated. Indeed, there seem to be no positive means of establishing in the foreseeable near term a *modus vivendi* between New Delhi and the Punjab. And, nearly three years after the Prime Minister accepted gracefully the massive victory of the Akali Dal in the Punjab State Elections of September, 1985, the situation has deteriorated to a point where the elected, but largely ineffective, government of the Akali Dal has been dismissed by the Centre and President's Rule has once again been instituted. The Sikhs remain fragmented in their own perceptions of what the future should be, virtually leaderless, and alienated from those who govern at the Centre. Sadly, violence, checked periodically by repressive "law and order" policies, is becoming institutionalized as the primary idiom of political expression in the continuing crisis.

CONTINUING PRESSURES
FOR REGIONAL AUTONOMY

During his first two and one-half years as Prime Minister, Rajiv Gandhi could not escape the need to address domestic political crises. And, though he earned high marks initially in India and elsewhere for the manner in which he dealt with the Punjab and similar issues (e.g., Assam)[28] characterized by their conspicuousness, it soon became obvious that his options would be limited and the implementation of his [presumed] choices impeded by political and economic considerations over which he had little control. It became apparent, even to those who wished the new Prime Minister well, that there would be

---

28. While the Prime Minister was praised widely for having negotiated "accords" in 1985 with dissenting groups in the Punjab and Assam, the subsequent electoral defeats of the Congress (I) in both states (and particularly in Assam in December of 1985) diminished the luster of his early record of achievement. With the loss in Assam, then the eighth state not ruled by the Congress (I), early euphoria in Congress circles concerning the "new generation of leadership" in India began to be replaced with concern about the Party's decline and Rajiv Gandhi's capacity to revitalize it.

no "quick fixes" for such crises. This still holds in 1988, especially for domestic crises that are linked to the on-going struggle in India between those who are pressing by diverse means for varying degrees of regional autonomy and those who see the need to preserve central authority over the states. Within this context Rajiv Gandhi's domestic policy initiatives have been, at best, qualified success stories -- to be perceived as damage control exercises, rather than as steps taken to resolve long-standing problems that continue to beset the political economy of India. His long-term success, if he is to experience it,[29] must be grounded in an ability to anticipate future headlines and to identify and deal with problems before they emerge as full blown crises of a sort that limit the options of any leader. What may be striking about the Punjab crisis is that it is not unique. The political and economic tap roots of the power struggle between the Centre and those pressing for an increase in regional autonomy extend into every region of the Republic, including the eastern region.[30]

One tap root is well-developed. It has been growing for more than thirty years -- ever since Rajiv Gandhi's grandfather, Jawaharlal Nehru, sanctioned the states' reorganization of India along linguistic lines in 1956. What may be lost in the discussion of "headline issues" that are associated with Center-state relations in the 1980s is the degree to which the states' reorganization according to

---

29. With the overwhelming defeat of the Congress (I) in the state elections in Haryana on June 17, 1987, the fifth state to vote against the Congress during Prime Minister Gandhi's tenure, opposition groups governed 11 of India's 25 states. The evident decline in the fortunes of Rajiv Gandhi's party during his watch has made him increasingly vulnerable to criticism within his own Party, and it is by no means certain that the Congress (I) will continue to recognize him as its leader.

30. It must also be emphasized that the issue of regional autonomy is not subsumed exclusively within the context of Centre-state relations. Many of India's states face similar pressures from within as subsets of people within their own boundaries, organized on ethnic, tribal, and linguistic bases, seek to establish their own separate identities. Such pressures are endemic in a plural society.

linguistic criteria in 1956 conferred legitimacy on all subsequent movements for regional autonomy, and weakened in principle the right of the central government to use its coercive power to exercise authority over the diverse peoples of India. It was implicit in the states' reorganization that the people of India, living in linguistic states, would have the right to evolve in ways consistent with local traditions and cultures. Thus, the decision in 1956 to transform the map of India to meet linguistic criteria confirmed India's pluralism and gave political legitimacy to what I have called subsequent movements for forms of regional autonomy.[31] If the pressures for various forms of regional autonomy in contemporary India were given political legitimacy by the states' reorganization of 1956, as I am suggesting, it may be useful to reflect now on the process by which Nehru and the Congress Party, at the height of their unitary power, conceded to that reorganization.

The redrawing of the map of India in 1956 was a momentous event in the modern history of India -- an event that was as transforming in its implications for the future structure of the system of governance in India as a whole series of constitutional amendments designed to weaken the authority of the Centre and to enhance the powers of the states. What is striking about this reorganization, together with its implicit transformation of the structure of power in India, is that it was endorsed by leaders who only a few years earlier had argued in the Constituent Assembly that the preferred system of governance would be that of a strong central government -- a government capable of exercising its authority over

---

31. This is not to suggest that the decision, necessarily and by itself, threatened the "unity" of India. Indeed, some have argued that India -- because all of its languages and dialects fall under four language groups (Indo-Aryan and Dravidian, and, to a lesser extent, Tibeto-Chinese, and Austro-Asiatic) that have been cross-fertilized by mutual borrowing -- is a single linguistic area. [See, for example, Murray B. Emaneau's article, "India as a Linguistic Area," in *Language*, 32, (1956).]

"the provinces" then, and now the "states."[32]   Moreover, the Founding Fathers of independent India had specifically resisted within the Constituent Assembly the proposition that India then be reorganized along linguistic lines, even though the Congress movement had been openly committed to, and its own internal organization based on, the principle of linguistic units.[33]   While it has been said that Jawaharlal Nehru believed that some kind of reorganization of the administrative units of the country would be inevitable, he was not prepared within the context of the Assembly to endorse a restructuring of the map of India along linguistic lines -- suggesting instead that such reorganization, should it take place, would appropriately emphasize "... cultural, geographic, and economic factors as well as language ...".[34]

As mentioned earlier, the clear intent of those who framed the Constitution of India -- imbued with an Indian "national" perspective, fresh from the divisive experience of the partition, comfortable in the nationwide authority of the Congress Party, and concerned about pressing issues of national import (e.g., how to establish sustained economic progress within a political economy ensuring distributive justice) -- was to ensure that the Central authority had transcendent powers over the constituent parts of the Union.   They thought that they were designing a system of governance based on "cooperative federalism" within which central authority would be predominant -- not a system of federalism in which the states would be encouraged to enlarge on powers conferred on them at the expense of the Centre.   As the members of the Constituent Assembly

---

32. As Granville Austin has earlier emphasized, there was a deep belief in the Assembly "... that the renascence of India demanded a strong central government."   And Nehru had said as early as 1936, as quoted by Austin, "It is likely that free India may be a Federal India, though in any event there must be a great deal of unitary control."   [For elaboration on this theme, see Granville Austin's *The Indian Constitution: Cornerstone of a Nation*, pages 186-207.]

33. Austin. *The Indian Constitution: Cornerstone of a Nation*. p. 243.

34. Ibid.

worked together to forge a constitution, they muted their own allegiances to "provincial" units of governance, and also made evident their rejection of a constitution based on Gandhian concepts of decentralization.[35]

The Constitution that emerged clearly reflected the dominant bias of those who drafted it. The central government, its constitutional authority reinforced and enhanced by sections on emergency powers, seemed on paper to be so potent in its authority that some worried about the residual powers of the provinces. Among these "worriers" were Rajendra Prasad and Pandit Pant -- already established as national leaders whose authority derived, in part, from strong provincial bases in the Hindi-speaking heartland of India. Rajendra Prasad, soon to become the first President of The Republic of India, held sway in Bihar. Pandit Pant was then the "Premier" of the United Provinces (soon to become Uttar Pradesh, the most populous and politically powerful of the modern states of India, mainly because of the size of its representation in Parliament). It is not surprising, given the subsequent independent strength of Uttar Pradesh in the Indian Union, that it was Pandit Pant who went on record against those in the Constituent Assembly who pressed for a strong central government. He spoke of the need for decentralized authority and warned against concentrating too much power at the Centre. Moreover, according to one account, Pant also argued, with prescience of the future dynamics of Centre-state relations, that it could not be assumed "... that the provinces can be made to cooperate against their own will by means of central legislation ...".[36] Clearly, Pandit Pant early understood that the Centre's capacity to initiate, or lead, could be blocked by the states' capacities to vitiate, and to refuse to follow.

If the record suggests that India's Founding Fathers actually opted for a strong Centre, ignored arguments concerning the need for decentralized authority, and opposed reorganization of the map of India along linguistic

---

35. Ibid., p. 188.

36. Ibid., p. 239.

lines, it is difficult to comprehend why the Government of India would accede only a few years later to changes that would in time enlarge the *de facto* powers and prerogatives of the states, raise questions about the authority of the Centre, and give legitimacy ultimately to those pressing in the 1980s for forms of regional autonomy. There can be, of course, no simple explanation for the shift in attitudes leading to the 1956 states' reorganization along linguistic lines. It is possible that the proponents of a strong central government were less dominant at the outset than the record suggests. Adherents within the Assembly to the view that linguistic provinces should be established were neither intimidated by those with whom they disagreed nor perceived by themselves or their adversaries to be "separatists" reluctant to accede to the central authority of the new state. To be for linguistic states carried no stigma. And, it is a significant measure of the latent strength of the proponents of linguistic states in the Constituent Assembly that, while conceding defeat, they secured the inclusion of a Constitutional provision (Article 3) by which the map of India could subsequently be redrawn without recourse to cumbersome procedures associated with the passing of constitutional amendments.

It seems evident, nonetheless, especially in retrospect, that the pressures for states' reorganization along linguistic lines could not have prevailed within the Constituent Assembly -- given its composition. Those assembled were mainly sophisticated nationalists, an educated, English-speaking elite, imbued with a sense of being Indian, rather than parochial Biharis, Bengalis or Madrasis. They were conscious of articulating "national goals."[37] And, while the members of the Assembly were surely representative of the "best and the brightest" who had led India to freedom, they were not fully representative of the diverse peoples of India. The great mass of the people, lacking political sophistication, but with a growing capacity to express their own needs, were not much in evidence. Nor were representatives of distinctive political groups: the Hindu Mahasabha, the Communist Party, and the Socialist Party.[38] The Assembly "... was a one-party body

---

37. Ibid., p. 21.

38. Ibid., p. 14.

in an essentially one-party country."[39]   Indeed, there were then no strong regional or provincially-based parties to press for forms of regional autonomy.[40]

This fact notwithstanding, the roots of states' reorganization along linguistic lines had already been established within the Congress Party itself. As mentioned above, the Congress had organized its own administration on the basis of linguistic units at its Nagpur Congress as early as 1920, and from then on had "... attacked as arbitrary and irrational the provincial boundaries drawn by the British."[41]   But, the principal impetus for linguistic states came as India's political participation deepened and became increasingly representative of a new, post-Independence generation of Indians whose habits of mind and valuations were deeply rooted in their own languages and cultures, rather than in enlightened nationalism and internationalism.

As the pressures mounted for linguistic states in the 1950s, some still spoke out against them -- suggesting that the change would be detrimental to the future unity of India.   Some warned that the advocates of linguistic states were endorsing new forms of communalism, and that, if the states were re-established along linguistic lines, caste rivalries would also be intensified.   For example, the demand (periodically enunciated) for a Mithila State (in north Bihar) could be interpreted adversely as a means mainly of enhancing the power in that locality of one community, Darbhanga Brahmans -- freeing them from competition in the larger context of Bihar with rival castes, notably Bhumihars and Rajputs.   Others suggested that the demands for new linguistic states, whatever their perceived legitimacy, would be divisive and of questionable value.

There were early warnings about the implications of states' reorganization along linguistic lines.   Selig Harrison, whose concerns were misinterpreted and depreciated by

---

39. Ibid., p. 9.

40. Ibid., p. 192.

41. Ibid., p. 240.

some, showed prescience in 1960 when, anticipating the subsequent growth of regional parties in India, he said that, "The great issue now on the anvil in India is whether representative institutions founded upon one implicit assumption, a national party system, will become an intolerable luxury in a political competition conducted between the central authority and regionally-based political forces."[42]

In the aftermath of states' reorganization, Harrison was also correct in pointing out that, while the formal constitutional authority of the Centre had not been weakened, the Centre's eventual weakness would result from the capacity of the states to resist central incursions.[43] This was his way of suggesting, as had Pandit Pant in the Constituent Assembly, that whereas the Centre could continue to articulate national goals within the range of its formal constitutional prerogatives, the states could not easily be compelled to support those goals actively, and could delay, deny and vitiate central initiatives.

Finally, while the states' reorganization in 1956 cannot be said to have given legitimacy to all movements for regional autonomy, including secessionist movements, it can be seen as a Nehruvian legacy that remains operative in 1988 -- one that tests the thesis that India's unity can best be preserved by permitting and ensuring its diversity. It is all the more striking then that Indira Gandhi spent a major portion of her time as Prime Minister doing her utmost to assert central authority and control over the states -- thereby, in effect, rejecting her own father's final vision of an India in which the constituent states would be given latitude to evolve within their own distinctive linguistic and cultural traditions.

The pressures for forms of regional autonomy continue unabated in contemporary India. Opposition leaders meet to discuss how best they can enlarge on the constitutional

---

42. Harrison, Selig S. *India: The Most Dangerous Decades.* (Princeton: Princeton University Press, 1960), p. 297.

43. Ibid., p. 298.

prerogatives of the states.[44]   Some Sikhs agitate for an independent Khalistan, while others search for the means of addressing grievances within the Indian Union.   Some Gurkhas call for their own "Gurkhaland" to be carved out of West Bengal,[45] while others serve loyally within prestigious units of the Indian Army.[46]   Less than one hundred thousand Kukis demand a state of their own in Manipur, while fewer than 50,000 Chakma tribesmen plead for the status of persecuted minorities in the new state of Mizoram.   The Jharkhand movement flourishes in southern Bihar.   The Bastar agitation persists in Madhya Pradesh, and the Hill State campaign in Uttar Pradesh has its own adherents.[47]

---

44. See, for example, the record of one such meeting in *Centre-State Relations*, edited by Sati Sahni (New Delhi: Vikas Publishing House Private Ltd., 1984).

45. The Government of India reached an "accord" with the Gurkhas in July of 1988.   Whether the accord has the effect of eliminating the Gurkhas's movement for regional autonomy remains to be seen.

46. Because there are more than 50,000 Gurkhas in the Indian Army, the "separatist" sentiments of some have implications that go beyond questions concerning whether and how they might establish their "regional identity".

47. Rajiv Gandhi's government has repeatedly sought to reach accords with regionally differentiated dissident or insurgent groups.   As this work was going to press, in August of 1988, the Government of India signed a peace accord with tribal insurgents in the northeast Indian state of Tripura. It was hoped that this new accord would end eight years of guerrilla warfare. The Tripura guerrillas had sought independence from India as a primary means of preserving their ethnic identity. Many of the tribespeople are Buddhists and Christians in a state where Bengali Hindus are now in the majority. "Under the Tripura accord, the rebels agreed to end their fight, deposit all their weapons, leave their hideouts and accept the Indian Constitution." [See the *New York Times* report entitled "India and Tribal Guerrillas Agree to Halt 8-Year Fight" by Sanjoy Hazarika, (August 13, 1988), page 3.] Similar accords have been signed with Sikh leaders in the Punjab in 1985, with student agitators in Assam in 1985, and with Mizo rebels in 1986. Meanwhile, the Naga insurgency in eastern India, which began in the 1950s, continues.

The political idiom of those striving for forms of regional autonomy varies, but there is a tendency for those pressing for a relaxation of central control to be stereotyped negatively by the Centre as extremists, terrorists, separatists, or secessionists. Meanwhile, it still seems evident that the vast majority of those demanding forms of regional autonomy seek no more, and no less, from the central government of India than was inherent in the 1956 decision to redraw the map of India to recognize and accept the country's pluralism -- a decision that endorsed the premise that India's unity would not be sought at the expense of its diversity.

In these circumstances, the challenge for the central government, whoever leads India, will be to respond to the various pressures for regional autonomy by diverse means. There can be no single policy established to meet different regional needs and demands. The critical task at the Centre will be to resist treating all who agitate for change in their rights and prerogatives as "enemies of the state" -- as persons committed to the dissolution of the Republic of India. The situation cries out for flexible, sensitive, widely differentiated government responses to those who challenge central authority. There must be a clear perception in New Delhi that the Centre's authority need not be asserted to direct or control every dimension of the political process in a plural society. There must be a clear perception in New Delhi that its authority in dealing with the states is not best established or maintained through the repeated use of coercive means.

There are few means of knowing how Rajiv Gandhi defines the role of the Center in relation to the states. It is possible that he will be reluctant to appreciate the essential legitimacy of the multiple movements for forms of regional autonomy that are presently active in India -- especially when those pressures are not everywhere expressed in extremist, secessionist, or violent terms. However, his behavior at the outset of his administration in 1985 suggested that he might be more flexible than his mother in dealing with groups pressing for forms of regional identity and autonomy. As noted earlier, he accepted gracefully electoral defeats in the Punjab and Assam, giving the impression that he might also accept the notion that his own prestige would not be diminished if he acceded to the demands of disparate groups in India's regions to set their own political agendas. But, as he (and his Party) suffered electoral defeats in 1987 in Kerala, in West Bengal and in Haryana, and as the killing persisted in the Punjab, it seemed increasingly likely that the Prime Minister would resort to *ad hoc* policies emphasizing law and order and repressive control by the Centre of dissenting regionalists. In the Summer of 1987, the politics of confrontation were ascendant, and the politics of accommodation and reconciliation seemed in danger of being abandoned. In the Summer of 1988, there were divergent trends: toward confrontation in the Punjab and toward accommodation in some other contexts, notably in reaching "accords" with militant Gurkhas in eastern India and insurgent tribespeople in the state of Tripura.

Irrespective of a leader's interests, capacities and propensities, Centre-state relations will remain a "persistent issue" in India -- challenging any leader to anticipate future headlines in that arena by ensuring that the country moves toward a system of governance that gives greater latitude to the states in the establishment of local and regional priorities in agricultural development, industrial development, in education, and in such other spheres as may in time seem appropriate (within or outside of the scope of Part XI of *The Constitution of India*, including what is known as the "Seventh Schedule", which specifies the functional divisions of authority between the central government and the states).

The unity of a plural society cannot be forced. It must be based in India on a system of governance that permits the evolution of independent leadership in the states, both within and outside of the Congress Party. It is increasingly evident that the unity of India requires the emergence of a new division of labor and authority between the Centre and the states. In some instances, particularly those defined by regionally differentiated needs and interests, the unity of India will require a progressive devolution of power from the Centre to the states. In other instances, for example those defined by national needs to preserve and protect individual rights of minority groups or by national development and security needs, the Centre will need to maintain and strengthen its authority. If the current system of governance in India is to be preserved, leaders at the Centre and in the states must find a means of accommodating both national and regional interests without resorting to the use of force. Failing such an accommodation, both national and regional leaders will learn most painfully that today's crises in the arena of Centre-state relations will be replicated tomorrow in bewildering variety and complexity as people in India's regions continue to press in different and increasingly militant ways for control over their own lives, for decentralization of power and for local autonomy.[48]

QUIET CRISES
IN BIHAR AND WEST BENGAL

The Case of Bihar

Notwithstanding the apparent need for a progressive devolution of power from the Centre to the states, there

---

48. In this section, I have not drawn illustrations from the South, where the pressures for regional identity and autonomy also abound. In this context, it must be remembered that the Congress (I) no longer has meaningful representation in the whole of South India. Power in the South has now, in effect, "devolved" from the Congress at the Centre, and is in the hands of regional parties. This fact will not prevent the emergence of new demands consistent (and inconsistent) with pressures elsewhere for forms of "regional autonomy". While Tamil leaders no longer talk of secession, they will continue periodically to express other, deeply imbedded, regional concerns-- for example, that the Centre is "imposing" the Hindi language on Tamil speakers through Doordarshan, the central government-controlled TV network. The fear persists among some in Tamil Nadu that the Centre is using Doordarshan as a means of ensuring that Hindi becomes, in time, the national language. [For an example of how this issue is articulated, see K.P. Sunil's article entitled "The Language Crisis" in *The Illustrated Weekly of India*, (June 2, 1985), pages 52-53.] Meanwhile, while "linguistic nationalists" in Tamil Nadu are perfectly willing to condemn the Centre's "interventionist policies" with respect to language, they are at the same time prepared to encourage the Centre to be interventionist in the affairs of neighboring Sri Lanka to protect a Tamil-speaking minority there. Such conflicting attitudes among regional interest groups toward the role of the central government in Indian affairs complicate policy decisions for those who govern at the Centre.

will be circumstances in future where no government at the
Centre will be able to ignore its own responsibilities for
creative action concerning problems not being adequately
addressed by the state or local authorities.   The State of
Bihar may well present such a challenge to the Centre.

In India, Bihar is a synonym for backwardness --
economic, social and political.   Moreover, in 1988 the State
of Bihar is widely perceived to be "virtually ungovernable."
The notion that Bihar is virtually ungovernable comes from
a Minister of State in the Government of Rajiv Gandhi, but
who made the point is unimportant.   There is no more
obvious fact in India than that Bihar is a state in which
civil authority is uncertain and in which violence is the
most certain means of getting someone's attention.

In Bihar, as in most agrarian societies, power derives
from control of land and, in independent India from the
days of Nehru on, Bihar's semi-feudal landlords have been,
at least nominally, "in charge" of events in that State.
While it was fairly widely suggested in the late 1970s and
early 1980s that the political economy of Bihar was being
transformed economically and politically with the seeming
emergence of backward castes, classified by some for
economic reasons as "middle peasants", in 1988 such
judgments can appropriately be classified as premature.
The mainly upper caste landlords remain at the apex of
Bihar's political economy.   Disputes over rights in land are
persistent and increasing in number.   Peasants who resist
the landlords tend to be referred to as Naxalites, giving
them a "leftist" or "extremist" patina that is often not
warranted, even though it can be said that some dissident
peasants in Bihar do belong to leftist groups -- a faction
of the Communist Party of India, Marxist-Leninist, the
Maoist Communist Center, and the Worker Peasant Struggle
Organization (*Muzdur Kisan Sangram Samiti*).   However, it
is as wrong to classify all dissident peasants in Bihar as
"ideological leftists or Naxalities" as it is to perceive
anti-government peasants in El Salvador uniformly as
"leftist guerrillas."   In Bihar, the almost official labeling
of peasant dissidents as Naxalites has become a convenient
means of justifying the use of repressive, counter measures
against them.   Thus, unsophisticated observers, whether
indigenous to India or foreign, can be encouraged to
accept official explanations of the need for the police to

use violent means against sections of the Bihar peasantry who, by imposed definition, can be said to be committed to the use of force to overthrow constitutional government.[49] A cottage industry in guns is well-established -- making it quite likely that the levels of violence will grow.[50] Intimidation and violence are the increasingly accepted means used by those at the bottom of the economic ladder as well as by those who control the land. Local power, *de facto* if not *de jure*, for the maintenance of law and order

---

49. While rural violence is a persistent theme in Bihar and has secured increasing press coverage in India in the 1970s and 1980s, there is seldom sophisticated analysis of the causes and nature of violent episodes. As noted in the main text, the use of labels ("Naxalite" and "extremist" having been established among popular code words) by both government and the media to describe differentiated subsets of people involved in violent acts tends to obscure what is actually happening in rural areas -- especially the socioeconomic roots of rural tensions that precipitate violent behavior. The evidence that I have gathered personally in Bihar over more than thirty years suggests that the greatest numbers of disputes leading to violence have economic origins and have to do with conflicts between "superiors" and "inferiors" over rights to land. In a sense, such disputes are caused by or associated with failed agrarian reforms -- reforms that raised expectations of profound change in the agrarian structure of Bihar, but did not deliver it. The process, begun in the 1950s, has contributed progressively over time to the capacities of the peasants, by themselves or with the assistance of others, to articulate their interests and to contribute to the State's political destabilization. Traditional landholders, fearing loss of land and power, have used every means over the last thirty-five years, legal and extra-legal, to deny substantive change in the agrarian structure. At the same time, poor peasants, lacking the means to challenge landholders successfully in courts of law, have gradually dared to employ their own extra-legal means to confront traditional authority and to assert their own rights to land. [For background and elaboration, see my 1974 analysis in *Agrarian Crisis in India: The Case of Bihar* (Austin and London: University of Texas Press, 1974).]

50. Guns are available in Bihar at prices that ensure their availability as never before to poor peasants who have grievances, and it has been reported that some peasant organizations are actually supplying the "disaffected" with homemade guns. [See, for example, Steven R. Weisman's piece in the *New York Times* entitled "India's Corner of Misery: Bihar's Poor and Lawless," (April 27, 1987).]

is increasingly in the hands of private armies of Mafia-type
goondas who employ violence themselves, or in association
with local police, to maintain the traditional authority of
the landed elites.[51]

Bihar's landed elites are also the state's political elite.
They control Rajiv Gandhi's Congress (I) in that state.
They are not now pressing for "regional autonomy"; they
have it.   They, or their ancestors, have exercised local
authority without the effective imposition of restraints by
any central authority for centuries.   New Delhi's authority
has not extended meaningfully into Bihar's countryside,
even during recent periods of President's Rule.

Thus, the pregnant question in Bihar has to do not
with whether the central government should grant
increasing autonomy to the state government in Bihar, but,
rather, with whether any supreme leader at the Centre can
permit this "ungovernable" state to continue as it is.
Bihar poses an obvious dilemma for Rajiv's Congress Party
and for the central government.   Should they intervene in
Bihar against the governing elite in a fashion that
contradicts recognition of the prime need in many other
states and regions of India to permit a "flowering of local
leadership" and forms of regional autonomy?   Or, should
they remain aloof from the situation in Bihar -- hoping
that the semi-feudal elites will continue to maintain power
without the negative headlines that could impel central

---

51. The reputation of Bihar as a lawless society is such that it is almost
fashionable for distinguished outsiders to intervene in the state's internal
affairs. For example, eleven months after police gunned down 23 apparently
unarmed peasants in the Bihar town of Arwal (on April 19, 1986), and the
local government had appeared to have bungled the subsequent investigation,
banned the peasants' organization (the Mazdoor Kisan Sangram Samiti) to
which some of those killed had belonged and labeled the victims as
"extremists", a body calling itself the Indian People's Human Rights
Commission came to the scene to gather evidence and to exert pressure on
those in Bihar who seemed reluctant to investigate the police firing. While
the Commission lacked legal authority, its members (including two former
justices of the Supreme Court of India and a former chief justice of the state
of Himachel) could be described as non-partisan. [For elaboration, see the
article entitled "Civil Rights: Championing a Cause," *India Today*, (March 31,
1987), p. 50.]

government involvement in the internal affairs of the state? It is not certain that Rajiv and his advisors at the Centre will have the vision, the courage, or the political power that would be needed to begin a process designed to change the political economy of Bihar -- enabling Bihar to become a national asset rather than a national liability.

The pressure for central government intervention in Bihar derives not only from that state's virtually ungovernable status, but also from the fact that Bihar has a rich and largely unrealized economic potential. From a technical agronomic point of view, Bihar, rather than the Punjab, should have been the modern breadbasket of India.[52] Yet, it persists in 1988 as a food deficit state in which substantial numbers of mainly low caste, landless peasants have experienced declining standards of living. What is more, the state is not totally lacking in a modernized industrial sector,[53] and is endowed with rich natural resources including uranium ore, iron ore, coal, copper ore, mica, together with fairly significant quantities of manganese, graphite, bauxite, limestone, and other minerals.

With all this potential, it is not surprising that Bihar has been rediscovered by the central government -- as well as by others.[54] For example, the Planning Commission

---

52. Numerous scholars have noted that Bihar's land and water resources are superior to those of the Punjab. The inhibiting variable concerning agricultural growth in Bihar has been the persistence of a semi-feudal system of agrarian relations -- a system that does not provide adequate incentives for economic innovation. [See, for example: Warriner, Doreen. *Land Reform in Principle and Practice*. (Oxford: Clarendon Press, 1969).]

53. There are heavy machine projects developed in collaboration with the Soviet Union in Ranchi, an oil refinery at Barauni, a uranium processing plant at Jadugudda, a Soviet-assisted steel mill at Bokaro, etc.

54. Among American institutions providing technical and economic assistance to India, there has been a belated recognition of Bihar's needs and potential. The Ford Foundation promoted modest-sized and largely exploratory efforts in agriculture and "social forestry" in Bihar in the 1980s. Also, the United States Agency for International Development (USAID) mission in India, having
(continued...)

focused attention on Bihar (and east India) in the Seventh Plan with a view toward strengthening that State's economy and addressing the problem posed by widening income inequality between the eastern region of India as a whole and other regions. Various expressions of interest in Bihar have not led, however, to a consensus concerning what is to be done there, if anything, and by whom.

Meanwhile, as noted above, the conditions of local violence and the use of unconstitutional force for the maintenance of law and order continue. And, to the extent that violence in Bihar remains endemic and local authority corrupt, pressures will mount on Rajiv Gandhi (or any subsequent leader at the Centre) to intervene. His options, especially as this quiet crisis deepens, are already narrowing and will continue to narrow unless he takes steps soon to anticipate "tomorrow's headlines." The rural violence in Bihar does not yet represent a coherent or organized peasant mobilization against the local ruling elites. However, it should be noted that the process of peasant mobilization is going on in Bihar in ways that have been observed elsewhere in rural areas in the twentieth century. For example, Steve Lohr, describing "insurgency" in the Philippines, argued that what happened there in 1985 was "home grown" and drew its strength from young people, "... the sons and daughters of impoverished tenant farmers ... who faced the same fate as their parents, working long hours to scrape a subsistence ... within a feudal agrarian world."[55] While there is no New People's Army in Bihar, the conditions for peasant mobilization in Bihar parallel those in the Philippines and in other

_____

54(...continued)

largely neglected Bihar for many years, expressed new interest in the State in 1986. In September of that year, the Mission Director in New Delhi told me that, "We [the USAID mission] shouldn't be here if we cannot do something in eastern India, and especially in Bihar." However, the USAID mission did not subsequently become active in Bihar, and, in any event, now plans (Summer of 1988) to curtail sharply or shut down its bilateral aid program in India.

55. Lohr, Steve. "Inside the Philippine Insurgency." *The New York Times Magazine.* (November 3, 1985), Section 6, p. 46.

societies that have already experienced, or are now experiencing, political instability supported by the new demands of the mainly illiterate sons and daughters of the rural poor. We have no way of predicting the pace of developments in Bihar. The coercive power of the local elites can keep the lid on probably for some time to come. However, if the central government fails to anticipate the headlines and fails to take action to correct the current state of affairs in Bihar, the prospect is that the Prime Minister will be asked, eventually, to send in the army to maintain the civil authority. If that happens, Rajiv Gandhi, or his successor, will be damned if he does employ the coercive power of the Centre and damned if he doesn't. In the meantime, the State's economic potential is not being realized.

The Case of West Bengal

In the preceding section on Bihar, we have examined (for illustrative purposes) a situation in which the political and economic pressures on Rajiv Gandhi may be such as to require central government intervention -- contradicting the apparent need in the nation as a whole for the Centre to permit various expressions of regional autonomy. Bihar's neighboring state, West Bengal, provides the Prime Minister with a different mix of Centre-state problems. In West Bengal the drive for regional autonomy is given expression by "Bengali nationalists" and the skillful manipulations of the Communist Party (Marxist).

The Communist Party (Marxist) in West Bengal has sought, with some success, to establish its political roots in the countryside. Prior to the 1970s, like most other Indian political parties, the Communist Party (Marxist) had drawn its strength mainly from urban areas, notably from Calcutta in West Bengal. However, since 1977, the Left Front Government of West Bengal has been adept at promoting a program of agrarian reforms designed to enable the Communist Party (Marxist) and its allies to establish a working nexus with segments of the rural poor, including scheduled castes, scheduled tribes, and *bargadars* (sharecroppers). The Left Front Government claims its greatest success in protecting and securing the rights of sharecroppers. Its Operation Barga, conceptualized largely by the Left Front's Land and Land Reforms Minister, Shri Benoy Chowdhury, and carried out with the active support of a civil servant of the Government of India (Land Reforms Commissioner, D. Bandyopadhyay), claimed to have registered the names of more than 1,296,000 sharecroppers through June of 1984. The registration of the names of *bargadars* is a means of providing the sharecroppers increased security on the lands traditionally tilled by them on the basis of oral leases from absentee landlords who could remove the sharecroppers from the land at will. It cannot yet be said that Operation Barga is a striking success, either as land reform or as a program designed to be the basis for rural economic progress in West Bengal. But, it surely is a political success because it has enabled the Left Front Government to establish its *bona fides* with an important constituency of the rural poor -- in a fashion not replicated elsewhere in India.

Moreover, the strategy of Operation Barga has been complemented by other programs of rural development, particularly ones designed to increase the area under irrigation as a means of facilitating economic growth. There were said to be 78,000 shallow tube wells in West Bengal in 1977 when the Left Front came to power. After ten years of Left Front rule, there were 225,000. Between 1977 and 1987 an additional 5.3 lakh hectares of land has been added to the area under minor irrigation.[56] And, while 65 percent of West Bengal's arable land remains unirrigated, the continuing investment in minor irrigation has already brought some positive results. In 1987, West Bengal became the second largest rice producer in India after the southern state of Andhra Pradesh.[57]

Meanwhile, well-publicized efforts have been made by the Government of West Bengal to secure improved wages for landless laborers and to give new strength and

---

56. In the thirty years from 1947-77, only 5.1 lakh hectares had been added to the total of irrigated land in the State. [Banerjie, Indranil. "The Red Stranglehold." *India Today*. (April 15, 1987), p. 46.]

57. Banerjie, Indranil. "The Red Stranglehold." *India Today*. (April 15, 1987), p. 46.

direction to village panchayat institutions. While it cannot be said in 1988 that rural Bengal has been transformed, the Left Front can claim to have established deep roots in the countryside. By providing direct benefits (improved shares of produce and enhanced security from eviction from lands tilled by them) to more than a million *bargadars* and by distributing eight hundred thousand acres of surplus farm land to 1.64 million recipients, the current Government of West Bengal has secured the support of substantial sections of the rural population. This was made evident in the Spring of 1987 during the West Bengal Assembly elections when the Left Front thrashed the Congress (I) -- with rural voters proving to be the key to the margin of victory.[58] The result must have been especially painful to Rajiv Gandhi because he campaigned vigorously in the state, drew large crowds, and put his own personal prestige on the line -- hoping, perhaps, that his own popularity would substitute for grass roots party organization.[59]

If Rajiv Gandhi and his party wish to reestablish their political influence in West Bengal, they will be faced with a choice between emulating the rural-based political strategy of the Left Front and continuing to place primary attention on the consumption and other needs of urban populations. It is possible that the Centre and the Congress Party (I) will decide virtually to concede the Left Front an "extended lease" on West Bengal -- recognizing that the costs of taking over the Government of West Bengal (and in the process having to take responsibility for economic progress and political stability in that State) may outweigh any benefits. West Bengal may be a case in which Rajiv Gandhi tactically can accept pressures for

---

58. The Left Front secured 251 seats and the Congress (I) only 40 out of a total of 294 seats in the State Assembly. [Banerjie, Indranil. "A Startling Sweep." *India Today*. (April 15, 1987), p. 44.]

59. While it has been apparent for some time that the Congress (I) has tended to rely on the popularity of its leader to secure votes, the Left Front in West Bengal is said to have a unit in every one of West Bengal's 41,000 villages, and almost nine million members out of a total population of 54 million. [Banerjie, Indranil. "The Red Stranglehold." p. 46.]

"regional autonomy" -- thus placing the direct burdens of governance on local opposition groups.

However, no central government of India can relish a situation in eastern India in which opposition groups are experimenting with rural-based strategies designed to give them "mass appeal" or in which the absence of sustained economic growth detracts from the national effort. The clear need is for the central government to determine its own course in West Bengal, as well as in Bihar, before its policy options are limited to *ad hoc* actions prompted by new headlines.

3

THE ARENA OF
THE NATIONAL ECONOMY

INTRODUCTION

From the beginning, after independence in 1947, India has articulated the need for sustained economic growth within a political economy ensuring social justice. These twin goals were to be achieved within the framework of democratic planning orchestrated by a centrally located, national Planning Commission. Five Year Plans, drafted by the Commission, would give direction and impetus to the economy. In time, India would thereby establish a socialistic pattern of society -- a society in which economic progress would be sustained within a more egalitarian social system. The embedded assumption in this vision of progress was that a *consensus universalis* concerning national needs and goals could be proclaimed at the Centre and implemented without coercion in a plural society bound to be driven by a whole panoply of different definitions of needs and interests. We now know, with the wisdom of hindsight, that this embedded assumption did not, in fact, apply. No Planning Commission at the Centre could establish a *consensus universalis* in a plural society simply by proclaiming it: not within a system of democratic governance where the responsibility for implementing plans and programs rested mainly with the states. No Planning Commission at the Centre could promote a socialistic pattern of society, even if it wished to do so, when the Founding Fathers had made plain that India would remain a society in which the private sector would be allowed to flourish -- irrespective of its characteristics.

Independent India's commitment to the establishment of a socialistic pattern of society was qualified and limited. The governing elite were in no way committed to abolishing the private sector -- even if it should prove to be an impediment to progress in India as some might define it. The whole of the agrarian sector and the whole of small industry were to remain in the private sector. Only critical "big industries" (e.g., iron and steel, mining, rail transport, defense industries, atomic energy, etc.) would be fostered within the public sector. It was understood that India would evolve as a "mixed economy" within which the private and public sectors would coexist.

Within the framework of her mixed economy, India achieved steady economic growth at an annual rate of roughly 3.5 percent between 1950-1951 and 1980-1981. An extensive industrial sector emerged (within a protected domestic economy) -- one that generates a wider array of products than most developing countries. Heavy industries have been established, providing a strong machinery sector within which large electrical generators, sophisticated machine tools, military hardware, chemicals and petrochemicals are produced. New colleges, universities and technological institutes have been promoted -- thereby ensuring that India would have a larger supply of skilled manpower (including scientists, engineers, and modern technicians) than any other country, excepting the United States and the Soviet Union. And, from the late 1960s, sufficient progress has been achieved in agriculture to ensure (by the 1980s) virtual self-sufficiency in the production of food and fiber.

These considerable achievements notwithstanding, it became fashionable in India in the late 1970s to question existing economic policies and to establish new directions. Even prior to the advent of the regime of Rajiv Gandhi, new policy initiatives were being considered to spur industrial growth and to improve productivity. It was widely suggested that steps had to be taken to encourage private investment in India, and to transform and limit the Government's industrial licensing system (by which the government had earlier sought to control which products a company might produce, and in what quantity). "Economic liberalization" had become a slogan, suggesting the need for new initiatives in the areas of industrial policy, trade policy, tax policy, and monetary policy.

NEW DIRECTIONS
IN THE SEVENTH PLAN

Coincident with the birth of the Seventh Plan (1985-1990), there was widespread conjecture concerning the future of economic planning in India. Some (including a few committed "social democrats" among India's ruling elite) feared that Rajiv Gandhi was prepared to eliminate whatever remnants existed of the "Fabian socialist" ideals that had been incorporated in the commitment to the use of "state planning" for development following India's independence. That commitment to state planning had become an article of faith in India -- an expression of nationalist fervor. It had been assumed for nearly forty years that large scale state intervention, coordinated in a plan, would be needed to ensure economic progress, and that giving free play to market forces would represent a post-independence capitulation to a particular brand of *laissez faire* that had been typical of the British colonial period.

It must be remembered that for many of the men who led India to freedom, and especially Rajiv Gandhi's grandfather, Prime Minister Jawaharlal Nehru, private enterprise and capitalism were associated with colonial domination and imperialism. For them, state planning and socialism seemed to offer a new, modern means of ensuring that political freedom would be followed quickly by economic progress leading to self-sufficiency. Economic self-sufficiency, they believed, would establish the basis for economic freedom. While it cannot be denied that Nehru and many other Indian intellectuals were influenced by the Soviet Union's earlier commitment to state planning, it is equally apparent that India's adoption of state planning as a means of promoting economic development was due ultimately to the ruling elites' basic perception of themselves as the historic decision-makers who knew best how to direct the upliftment of countrymen too poor and backward to know how to help themselves.[1]   This basic perception was consistent with the subliminal notion, still prevalent in India in 1988, that economic progress could be achieved in India -- even within a political system embracing universal adult franchise -- in a fashion that would not threaten elite dominance.

Notwithstanding this background, it became apparent in 1985 that the commitment to state planning was being challenged.   The Planning Commission was no longer recognized as the prime instrument of public policy formation.   New directions were being formulated outside of the Commission either by L.K. Jha or by other economic advisers.   These advisers -- including applied economists previously working for multilateral institutions such as the World Bank and the International Monetary Fund (IMF) -- enjoyed the confidence of the new Prime Minister.   It seemed that India was prepared to liberalize its economy and to embrace free market principles in order to spur higher rates of economic growth than had been achieved through the mechanism of state planning.

The atmosphere was one of critical introspection concerning economic policy and priorities.   There was fairly widespread concern that India's long-term rate of economic growth was insufficient to meet national needs. And, irrespective of changing policy emphases over time, the country seemed capable of sustaining a long-term rate of growth of around only 3.5 percent -- what Professor Raj Krishna called somewhat despairingly "the Hindu rate of growth."[2]   What was needed was a much higher rate of

---

1. It is wrong, in any event, to suggest that the Congress Party, after Independence, was comprised of committed socialists.   While the Party has undoubtedly included a broad spectrum of interests, its disposition has been conservative.   The Party's language and rhetoric have always been more radical in tone than its actual policies -- particularly in rural areas where there has been consistent support for traditional landholders' rights to private property in land.

2. In recent years, the trend rate of growth in India has in fact been higher than 3.5 percent.   According to The World Bank, India's average annual growth rate was 3.9 percent in the period 1965-1973 and somewhat higher (an

(continued...)

economic growth (possibly as high as seven percent per annum until the turn of the century) if India were to meet its old objectives of eradicating poverty and of limiting or ending dependence on external financial assistance.

Reflecting on India's economic achievements and future prospects, L.K. Jha suggested in December of 1986[3] that India was not using capital efficiently -- that its incremental capital to output ratio was too high (i.e., that India was using too many units of capital to produce a unit of output). By that measure, both Pakistan and Bangladesh, with lower incremental capital output ratios than India, were using capital more efficiently than India. While Jha went on to suggest that India could derive satisfaction from its considerable economic achievements since independence (especially given the country's need to maintain high levels of defense expenditure to meet perceived external threats, and to spend large sums on relief and welfare in the interests of social justice), he argued that without any additional resource mobilization, but with improved management and utilization of existing resources, the country could achieve a growth rate of seven percent or more from the Seventh Plan period on to the turn of the century.

Jha further argued that the very fact that India had been short of capital had, paradoxically, caused the country to rely excessively on capital as the principal resource in development projects. In the process, insufficient attention had been accorded to "land" and "labor" -- important resources that were not as scarce as capital.

Jha's observations were especially pertinent to the early history of economic planning in India when, during the first three Five Year Plans, insufficient attention was

---

2(...continued)

average of 4.1 percent) from 1973 to 1984. [See page 182, Table 2., "Growth of Production," in *World Development Report 1986*, published for The World Bank by Oxford University Press.]

3. See the text of Mr. Jha's "Govind Ballabh Pant Memorial Lecture," delivered on December 10, 1986, in New Delhi under the auspices of the Govind Ballabh Pant Memorial Society and the India International Centre, as reported in *The Times of India*, December 31, 1986.

given to policies designed to increase the productivity of the land. Clearly, at the outset, the Government of India did not accord a high enough priority to agriculture, and did not become sufficiently aware of the need for investment in agriculture until it became apparent in the late 1960s that food shortages might have political and social, as well as economic, costs for the nation.[4] When agriculture was finally given some priority in the late 1960s, in the face of food shortages and agrarian unrest, it provided a critical boost for the Indian economy -- leading to an improvement in the overall rate of growth, even when the rate of industrial growth was declining.

As the debate over public policy and state planning continued, additional voices were raised -- reflecting, for example, persistent tensions between the states and the central government in the setting of national priorities, and the growth of regional centers of opposition to the Congress Party (I). In this context, the Janata Party leader, Ramakrishna Hegde, Chief Minister of the southern state of Karnataka, questioned India's achievements over six five year plans and suggested that the primary accomplishment had been the creation of two Indias: a prosperous India, characterized by high technology and sophisticated industries, and a traditional India, steeped in poverty, unemployment, hunger, disease and illiteracy. Hegde went on to challenge the very process of state planning in India, suggesting that there was insufficient involvement of the states in determining the nation's strategies and priorities.[5]

Others weighed in to endorse the planning process in India, to welcome the "realistic" look of the Seventh Five Year Plan, and, at the same time, to make critical observations concerning Prime Minister Rajiv Gandhi's "New Economic Policy" (with its rhetorical emphasis on economic efficiency, competition and modernization). While noting

---

4. See, for example, "The Causes and Nature of Current Agrarian Tensions," (New Delhi: Government of India, Ministry of Home Affairs, 1969). This report, though unpublished, was widely circulated.

5. For elaboration on Ramakrishna Hegde's theme, see the January 8, 1987 issue of the *Business Standard*, published in Bombay.

that cynics might ascribe the new emphases as having been conferred on India by the World Bank and the International Monetary Fund, rather than by India's Planning Commission, Mr. I.G. Patel, suggested[6] that the New Economic Policy had its own independent adherents who had long recognized that Indian economic development had been inefficient in the sense that the returns on the vast amounts of investment made over nearly four decades had been less than expected. The rate of saving and investment in India had been high (for a poor country), but the rate of growth had been low. In this context, Patel welcomed new policies that would reduce the Indian economy's reliance on government subsidies, controls and licenses and subject Indian industry to the forces of competition. He associated increased efficiency in the Indian economy with policies that would free industry "... from the shackles of industrial licensing,[7] import and other forms of control such as price control or controls exercised ostensibly to overcome regional imbalance or monopoly and restrictive practices, or that peculiarly Indian invention, viz, concentration of economic power."[8] Said Patel, "Even those of us who had actively promoted the earlier policies of the fifties and the early sixties have come to realize for some time now that we had underestimated the long-term deleterious effects of controls and had not appreciated sufficiently the potential for a self-serving alliance between political leaders and civil servants on the one

---

6. For a more detailed exposition of Mr. I.G. Patel's observations concerning India's "New Economic Policy", see his "Kingsley Martin Memorial Lecture" delivered at Cambridge, England, on November 5, 1986, as reported on November 6, 1986 in India's *Economic Times*.

7. With reference to industrial licensing, Patel bluntly asserted that "It has not reduced concentration of economic power or prevented the spread of luxury consumption or checked the wastefulness of unnecessary duplication of effort. On the contrary, it has often sanctified such waste through a desire to spread the favours around and compounded it by nurturing uneconomic scales of production all along the line." [Ibid.]

8. Patel, I.G. "Kingsley Martin Memorial Lecture," at Cambridge, England on November 5, 1986.

hand and captains of industry or the large farmers who
have sufficient clout both socially and financially on the
other. This diagnosis, I believe, is largely shared by
critics from the Left as well."[9]

Having commended certain emphases of the New
Economic Policy in India, Mr. Patel also expressed some
strong misgivings about them. He said that the new
initiatives, by placing great emphasis on "economic
efficiency", might convey the impression that the New
Economic Policy was "... at best neutral in relation to
considerations of equity or equality. It gives to the
opposition from the Left the monopoly of raising the flag
of equality and of creating the impression that Mr. Gandhi
and his colleagues are about to dismantle the socialist
legacy of Jawaharlal Nehru and Indira Gandhi. The truth
of the matter is that there was nothing particularly
socialistic or egalitarian about the earlier license-
permit-subsidy Raj which, in fact, helped to protect the
turf of powerful vested interests and heaped on them the
additional reward of much unearned rent as recompense for
political and financial support."[10] The emphasis on
efficiency, Patel added, would mean little unless it was
linked to steps to promote integrity in public life: the
reduction of "... corruption and the consequent inequitable
distribution of the costs and benefits of development."[11]

Patel went on to argue that there was more to
fostering economic efficiency than is commonly found in
the text-books of economists. He warned that economic
policies aimed at increasing the efficiency of production
could be offset by a continuing law and order problem in
the country, and he suggested also that it would be a
mistake if the country continued to downgrade the
importance of planning functions and the Planning
Commission itself. After all, he said, even if market forces
were given new importance in India, a vast amount of

---

9. Ibid.

10. Ibid.

11. Ibid.

investment in social and economic infrastructure would still have to be "planned."

Finally, Patel suggested that the New Economic Policy of deregulating or freeing the industrial economy, however desirable it might prove to be in the long-run for the economy as a whole, would do nothing in the short-run to provide more employment in rural areas or to reduce poverty in general. In political terms, from Patel's perspective, the new policy emphases would leave vast sections of the society virtually untouched. He concluded by suggesting that the economic liberalization policies would be unlikely to gain sufficient support within India unless they were designed and implemented in a fashion which would ensure simultaneous renewed emphasis on anti-poverty programs. Said Patel, "The introduction of computers and the newer technologies on a much larger scale by facilitating their import or production at home has obvious relevance for the rather small sector of organized industry or telecommunications, banking and the like. But it is not easy to see what relevance all of that has to the life of the small and marginal farmer or the landless rural worker ...".[12]

The preceding paragraphs will have confirmed, at least, that Indians themselves have found it difficult to reach consensus concerning the policy perspectives that were put forth in the Seventh Five Year Plan and its associated "doctrines." Consensus-reaching concerning India's Five Year Plans is always difficult because the Plans embrace multiple agendas for action, and cannot be expected to be implemented in fine detail as written.

What was clear in the Summer of 1988 was that the Government of India has found it necessary to retreat from much of the language, if not all of the content, of economic liberalization, and to confirm its adherence -- if only for rhetorical flourishes in elections -- to socialist principles. In other words, economic policy in India remains, as usual, in flux -- and the Seventh Plan itself is even less likely to be implemented as written than earlier plans. This could be said, even if it were clear that a consensus had been reached -- even among Indian

---

12. Ibid.

economists -- on the strategy of development to be pursued for the remaining years of the Plan.

Beyond this, the Seventh Plan may be quite unrealistic, as originally written. The World Bank estimated that the Seventh Plan would call for a rough doubling of the gross capital inflow into India from $17.5 billion to $34.5 billion during the plan period. This, in turn, would imply that India would have to enter into commercial loan commitments on the order of $4.5 billion a year during the Seventh Plan period. It remains to be seen whether India will in fact engage in that amount of commercial borrowing -- especially when there are said to be strong currents within the Government of India recommending against such an approach.

Setting aside concerns about how the plan is to be financed, the greatest speculation is whether Rajiv Gandhi, no longer basking in the glow of his "honeymoon" period, can retain sufficient control of his Party and the civil service to effect an economic strategy designed to a) embrace "free market" principles;[13] b) stimulate exports, even in the face of protectionist sentiment in the United States and elsewhere;[14] c) open the economy to foreign investment; d) give emphasis to high technology as the means of ensuring rapid economic growth; e) curb the often capricious administrative authority of an entrenched bureaucracy as it deals with the private sector in India and potential foreign investors; and f) cater to the consumption interests and needs of India's urban educated elites.[15]

---

13. The Seventh Plan still employs old rhetoric in support of the public sector, but for the first time ever the public sector will get less than one-half of the total projected investment outlay. The total investment outlay over the five-year period was expected to be Rupees 3.22 trillion at 1984-1985 prices; the public sector was expected to generate 48 percent of that total.

14. A version of the draft plan anticipated Indian exports growing at the rate of 13 or 14 percent per annum in the Plan period -- a most optimistic and unlikely eventuality.

15. The consumption needs, interests, and capacities of India's mainly urban,

(continued...)

This is an enormous agenda -- and one that seems to abstract from the needs of the majority of the people of India who remain dependent on agriculture for survival.[16]

Some sections of the Seventh Plan have a Utopian flavor. The Plan looks ahead to the year 2000 with great optimism -- anticipating that only five percent of the Indian population (i.e., only forty-nine million out of nearly one billion people) will then be below the official poverty line, when, in 1985, there were 36.9 percent living below the poverty line (as defined by the Government of India). While India has shown a stable growth rate over the last three decades (at about 3.5 percent per annum),[17] this low rate of long-run economic growth has allowed only a 1.3 percent rate of growth in per capita income. If such a trend rate of growth were projected through the rest of the decade of the 1980s and the 1990s, India's per capita income (approximately $260 in 1985) would be only $328 in the year 2000. Such a performance would clearly be unacceptable if India really hopes to reduce poverty as projected in the Seventh Plan. It has been estimated that India would need to sustain an aggregate growth rate of

---

15(...continued)

educated "middle-class" have been growing rapidly. Within this general category, there are now at least thirty million households in India (representing roughly 120 million people) with average annual incomes of US$2500 or more. These people constitute an important market for consumption goods -- a market that is expanding quickly in the 1980s.

16. While there has been a structural change in the Indian economy over the last forty-one years, reducing the share of agriculture from roughly 60 percent to an estimated 32.7 percent by the end of the Seventh Plan in 1990, no contemporary student of India's political economy can afford to forget that more than two-thirds of the Indian people continue to be dependent on agriculture for their main means of livelihood.

17. Despite a relatively low rate of GDP growth in 1987-1988 (i.e., 1.9 percent, when India experienced what has been described as the worst drought in over a century), GDP growth in 1988-1989 is expected to be in the neighborhood of 5 percent. The hope is that GDP growth will reach 6 percent in the last year of the Seventh Plan, 1989-1990.

about 5 percent per annum over the fifteen years from 1985 to the year 2000 before poverty would begin to diminish. And even this rate of growth would produce an Indian per capita income of only $574 by the year 2000. Moreover, it should be noted that the Government of India's own official statistics suggested in 1978 that between 309 million and 371 million people were then below the poverty line, and the Sixth Plan mentioned a figure of 320 million. If the numbers below the poverty line are projected at the same rate as seemed to be documented in the Sixth Plan, "... there will be 390 million Indians below the poverty line in the year 2000."[18] What is striking about this projection is that it establishes the possibility that there will be more people below the poverty line in India in the year 2000 than there were Indians alive at the time of Independence from Britain in 1947. Whether we adhere to the optimistic expectations of the future that are put forth in the Seventh Plan or prefer the rather dismal scenario outlined above, it seems clear that there will be a persistent need for sustained increases in economic growth at rates much higher than have been achieved in the past if India is to meet the minimum needs of a still rapidly growing population -- not to mention reducing significantly the numbers of people below the official poverty line.

PERSISTENT ISSUES
IN THE RURAL ECONOMY

Quite apart from the general direction and thrust of India's Seventh Five Year Plan, there is a tendency in contemporary India to take for granted the success achieved in agriculture. Agriculture has been a sector with a stable growth rate of around 2.6 percent per annum. This was achieved prior to the so-called Green Revolution by increasing the area under cultivation and after the

18. The quotation is from an unpublished paper, "The Economic Outlook for India", of the late Professor Raj Krishna, one of India's leading economists. [An edited version of this paper was published as Chapter 9 in *India 2000: The Next Fifteen Years*, James R. Roach editor (Riverdale, Maryland: The Riverdale Co., Inc., 1986).] Raj Krishna died in Rome in May of 1985.

introduction of new technology in the 1960s by increasing the intensity of cultivation. India's planners clearly hope that this rate of annual growth can be maintained during the Seventh Plan and beyond.[19] Indeed, such a rate of growth in agricultural production -- if maintained until the year 2000 -- is considered sufficient to meet India's food requirements in the early years of the twenty-first century (whether measured in subsistence amounts at 385 grams per day per capita or at a proposed higher maximum per day of 500 grams).

What is troubling about such discussions of agriculture's role in the Indian economy is that they emphasize aggregate indicators of performance and of needs. So long as we use aggregate measures of success, it is possible to commend India for having achieved self-sufficiency in the production of food grains (and even surpluses available for export). However, when our measures of success are no longer aggregative, we are likely to perceive persistent problems in states that are not self-sufficient in the production of food grains (e.g., Bihar and West Bengal) and that must receive monthly shipments from central reserve stocks. What is more, as soon as we cease relying on aggregate measures of success for the nation as a whole, even India's acclaimed Green Revolution loses much of its luster. The Green Revolution needs to be perceived as a "qualified success story." While wheat production nearly trebled, rice production rose by only 16 percent. As is well known, the preferred food grain in East India is rice. This is another way of noting that the primary benefits of the Green Revolution, even when measured in production aggregates, were regionally differentiated. Moreover, there is a tendency for some

19. In this context, it should be noted that India's agricultural production has not been particularly encouraging in the 1980s. The growth of agricultural production has averaged roughly 1 percent per annum, and there have been sharp declines in production in 1986-1987 and 1987-1988 as a result of successive droughts. Notwithstanding modern investments in irrigation over more than three decades, India's agriculture remains, even in the 1980s, critically dependent on the vagaries of the annual monsoon.

economists to forget that the "new strategy in agriculture" associated with the so-called Green Revolution is now recognized to have conferred its benefits within regions mainly on peasant cultivators with secure rights in land (classified appropriately enough in the West as landowners). Throughout India, it is those who have secure rights in land who "... have gained relative to tenants and laborers from the adoption of the higher yielding grain varieties."[20] It is this fact which highlights the great failure of independent India to establish and maintain a strategy for rural development linked to and based on the prior implementation of agrarian reforms. It is this failure, more than any other, that threatens the long-term stability and viability of the Indian political economy. And, it is to the description and analysis of this failure within the agrarian sector that I shall devote attention in the remaining pages of this chapter.

By focusing almost exclusive attention on India's agrarian sector (and the failure of agrarian reforms within that sector), I realize that I am abstracting from a whole host of persistent economic issues in the domestic economy. Nonetheless, I have chosen to focus on the agrarian sector because: (a) it remains the sector within which the majority of Indians must subsist; (b) it is the sector within which progress since independence has been most widely proclaimed; and (c) it is a sector within which there is great discrepancy between the success achieved (measured in production aggregates for the nation as a whole) and the actual distribution of direct benefits among different sections of the peasantry. Point (c) has particular cogency if India is, indeed, a plural society within which "progress" should not be defined only in aggregative production terms.

---

20. Ruttan, Vernon W. "The Green Revolution: Seven Generalizations." *International Development Review.* (December, 1977), pp. 16-22.

Agrarian Reforms Disassociated
from Agricultural Development

The disassociation of land reform, and agrarian reforms[21] generally, from agricultural development policy can be explained variously, and summarized at the outset in a few declarative statements. Each of these four statements will be elaborated in succeeding sections. First, it is significant in my view that the agrarian reform legislation enacted in the Indian states was drafted mainly by civil servants in revenue ministries, rather than by those in other ministries of government directly charged with agricultural development. Accordingly, the generalization can be made that the most meaningful segments of the legislation initially passed in India after independence in the name of "land reform" should be characterized instead as "revenue reform" -- a means of rationalizing and defending within the framework of the Constitution the states' right to act as "super-landlords" in the direct collection of land revenue.

Second, such legislation as was enacted was antithetical to the interests of India's landholding elites, who therefore sought every means at their disposal, legal and extra-legal, to nullify the significance of the reforms, and to delay their implementation -- while at the same time searching for means of ensuring economic progress in rural areas in ways that would not threaten their own traditional places at the apex of the agrarian hierarchy of interests in land.

Third, the ruling Congress Party lacked the political will to legislate and implement agrarian reforms, perceiving correctly that such reforms, if effected, might weaken the

---

21. "Land reform" is used here to suggest basic changes in the distribution of rights in land. It is a term used narrowly to refer to changes in the agrarian structure that shift control of land resources from one landholder to another. The term "agrarian reforms" is used here to refer to a constellation of initiatives designed to effect changes in traditional institutions pertaining to rights in land in India. Thus used, "agrarian reforms" is a comprehensive term embracing "land reform" and applying also to *zamindari* or landlord abolition, "ceilings legislation," "consolidation of holdings," or other such reform programs initiated in the Indian states over the last forty-one years.

Party's political roots in the countryside. Accordingly, the Party repeatedly employed the language of reform (articulating the need for social and distributive justice and the banishment of poverty) as a substitute for action. Lacking consensus within its own ranks concerning how agricultural development policy might be defined and implemented to satisfy the twin needs of increases in production and improved distribution of what was produced among the people, the Party resorted to strategies (endorsed by the international community) that suggested that these production and distribution needs could be addressed adequately in sequence over time, emphasizing productivity increases first, rather than simultaneously.

Fourth, key players[22] in the international community who were committed to assisting India's economic development consistently gave low priority to agrarian reforms as part of a strategy for addressing poverty issues and pursuing rural economic development. In time, indigenous elites and international donors of foreign economic and technical assistance -- each, for different reasons -- would coalesce in a strategy for rural development that would abstract from the agrarian structure of India as it was and focus primarily on the achievement of aggregate production increases in agriculture by applying new technology in that sector.

Agrarian Reforms Divorced
from Agricultural Policy Issues

The dichotomy between agrarian reforms and agricultural policy is made plain by a survey of such agrarian reform legislation as was enacted. As one reads the volumes of such legislation enacted by the Indian states, it is striking that the reforms have been largely

22. The reference to "key players in the international community" is, essentially, to The Ford and Rockefeller Foundations together with the United States Agency for International Development. This theme will be elaborated in a subsequent section of this chapter entitled "Agrarian Reforms Discouraged by Foreign Aid Institutions."

divorced from purposes associated with agricultural development. The commonalities in the legislation have something to do with modifying traditional "rights in land" to ensure, vaguely, that the "traditional agrarian structure" will neither impede economic progress nor ensure that the benefits of economic progress are conferred mainly on traditional landholders. Yet, detailed examination of the legislation makes plain that the legislation, as drafted and enacted into law within India's states, was virtually an end in itself. Little attempt was made to associate the legislation, or to link it either directly or indirectly, with specific complementary programs designed to contribute to the efficiency and productivity of agriculture. Whether we find merit or not in the actual provisions of the agrarian reforms enacted in the Indian states since independence, any analysis of the content of that legislation would support the judgement that very little effort was expended to ensure that the reforms were linked conceptually to programs of rural economic development.

In specific content, the reforms reflected, inevitably, the interests of those who framed them. In this context, it is important to remember, as noted earlier, that the actual "framers" (as distinct from those legislators who ensured that there would be sufficient "loopholes" in the laws to protect the interests of the landholding elite in rural areas) were mainly civil servants in the states' revenue ministries. We should not be surprised in retrospect that their focus, more often than not, was on reforms that would rationalize -- and not necessarily diminish -- the collection of land revenue. Thus, for example, the emphasis of "land reform" in the Permanent Settlement Region of eastern India was on removing "intermediaries" (otherwise classified as landlords or *zamindars*) roles in the collection of land revenue, and replacing the intermediaries with "state collectors" who would establish a direct nexus between the state and the cultivating peasantry in the collection of land revenue.

Agrarian Reforms Delayed
and Denied in Implementation

Concerning the enactment and implementation of agrarian reforms, it must be remembered that agriculture was and is a state subject under the Constitution. Thus, even if the political will to implement meaningful reforms could have been assumed at the Centre, this alone would not have ensured implementation of the reforms in the states. In this sphere of public policy, the states of India reigned supreme -- and continue in 1988 to reign supreme. And, because the agrarian histories of the states (together with their historical land systems) varied throughout the country, it was inevitable that the states would enact and implement different laws reflecting local conditions. It was also inevitable that the laws would reflect varying degrees of local political will to transform the traditional land systems. In any event, the cumulative record of legislation for agrarian reforms suggests that few states (the possible exceptions from some perspectives being Kerala and, more recently, West Bengal) have showed much interest in passing and implementing laws designed to change traditional agrarian structures. Not surprisingly, when laws were passed, they frequently contained carefully crafted loopholes designed to limit the impact of the legislation on traditional landholders, and some others having clearly delineated interests in land. Meanwhile the persistent power of landholders in the Indian political economy (impressed directly on sections of the peasantry by coercive means and indirectly, but no less conclusively, in the courts on those occasions when their rights to land were questioned) helped to ensure that the old order would not entirely disappear. When necessary (particularly following spates of legislation designed to put a "ceiling" on the size of landholdings) these direct and indirect means of preserving landholders' power were augmented by neat gambits -- for example, the obfuscation of land records by means of *benami*, or fictitious, transfers of land, either to family members and distant relatives or other persons and animals, living or dead.

It is quite evident from the record that such reforms as were legislated in the various states (whatever their intrinsic merits on paper) were delayed in implementation.

We need not cite here in any detail the means employed by landlords (prolonged litigation in the courts, delays in updating land records, the use of loopholes in the laws to retain land for "personal cultivation," the coercive eviction of cultivators from lands customarily tilled by them, *benami* transfers of rights in land to evade ceilings legislation, etc.) to delay the implementation of reforms. What is clear, and has been evident for years, is that agrarian reforms in India have, in the general case, been both delayed over the last forty years and denied. It is axiomatic in this arena of public policy that reforms that are delayed are by definition reforms denied.

Though implementation of agrarian reforms has been, with few exceptions, delayed and denied at the state level, the rhetoric of agrarian reforms still persists at the Centre. Today, agrarian reforms exist as a policy "residual" in the Five Year Plans, even though, so far as I know, they have few adherents in the central government, and probably even fewer in most of the states of the Union. The Seventh Five Year Plan has again reiterated standard recommendations in this sphere of public policy -- suggesting in fifteen numbered paragraphs over two pages that agrarian reforms[23] will be an intrinsic part of the Plan's anti-poverty strategy.

In the fashion that has become both customary and, one fears, devoid of serious intent, the states are exhorted in the Plan to enact laws, if they have not already done so, to secure the rights of tenants and to regulate rent. It is further suggested that this process be expedited by organizing "quick surveys" for recording and registering tenants, as well as protecting tribals and scheduled castes from the further alienation of their lands.

The states are also encouraged to get on with the business of distributing "surplus lands" (derived from the partial implementation of "ceilings laws" limiting the size of holdings) to the "landless poor." The Plan also makes plain in this context that at least 1.6 million acres of such surplus lands are the subjects of litigation, and urges action under Article 323B (the 42nd Amendment) of the

---

23. In fact, the Plan uses the term "land reform." I am substituting "agrarian reforms" in the text because it is the encompassing term used in this essay.

Constitution to remove remaining impediments to the distribution of those lands.

State governments are advised to take over surplus lands that cannot be distributed because they are "unfit for cultivation" in order to ensure their development "in a planned manner". Schemes for providing financial assistance to recipients of surplus land are to be continued -- and these recipients are to be given priority aid within the context of other initiatives of government, including the Integrated Rural Development Program.

Consolidation of holdings, according to the Plan, having not made much headway in many states, is also to be given some priority in the Seventh Plan period, particularly in the eastern region of the subcontinent where a "Special Programme for Rice Production" is to be taken up. The Seventh Plan reports that 5.6 million hectares were consolidated in the Sixth Plan and the total of consolidated acreage in the country at the beginning of the Seventh Plan was estimated to be 51.8 million hectares -- representing roughly one-third of the total cropped area of the country.

There is also the perennial recognition in the Plan of the need in India for up-to-date land records if agrarian reforms of all kinds are to be properly implemented. I would like to emphasize, here, that this "need" for up-to-date land records has been used for decades as a seemingly legitimate means both to explain the slow implementation of agrarian reforms and to delay their implementation. There was no "need" for such records, and the lengthy cadastral surveys that precede their updating, to effect land reforms in Japan. And, there was no "need" for independent India to continue to employ cumbersome British colonial procedures in order to update land records in preparation for the enactment and implementation of agrarian reforms. Nevertheless, as a means of encouraging the updating of land records, the Seventh Five Year Plan proposed that a "Centrally Sponsored Scheme" be implemented on the basis of matching contributions by the states and the Centre for that purpose.

Such Seventh Plan recommendations for "land reforms," couched as they are within the framework of exhortations and permissive incentives, are unlikely to be acted upon with vigor by the states -- especially when the states, eleven of which now have non-Congress (I) governments, are even more prone than in the past to disdain central government advice and direction. Such recommendations in themselves do not convey with any force a sense that the will exists in New Delhi to make agrarian reforms a meaningful instrument of public policy associated with alleviation of rural poverty. In effect, the recommendations in the Seventh Five Year Plan with respect to agrarian reforms reconfirm the practice of expressing commitment to an ideal without also establishing how, precisely, that ideal is to be fulfilled.

Agrarian Reforms Thwarted
by Ambiguous Commitment

If agrarian reforms have largely failed in India, that failure can best be understood by analysis of the peculiar nature of the national commitment to such reforms. That commitment has deep roots in the past. Among the goals enunciated by the Congress movement prior to independence was that of "comprehensive" agrarian reforms. It was easier then, as now, to reach apparent consensus on the need for such reforms than it was to make explicit the meaning of agrarian reforms to various interest groups within the Congress coalition, and to confirm their relevance either to agricultural development policy or poverty alleviation in the countryside. For some, particularly westernized intellectuals within the movement, the general commitment to agrarian reforms was associated loosely with the development of a socialist India in which the ideals of equality and social justice might be realized. Within the Congress, the most committed to radical reforms, including basic land reforms leading to a redistribution of rights in land in the countryside, were the Congress Socialists, [24] who, prior to independence, included men such as Jaya Prakash Narayan and Rammanohar Lohia. Occupying a position apart from this group, but expressing similar intellectual commitment concerning the need for agrarian reforms, was Jawaharlal Nehru. These proponents

---

24. The Congress Socialists were established within the Congress in 1934.

of agrarian reforms tended to see them, vaguely, as having symbolic and extended meaning; for them agrarian reforms were to be part of a still nebulous program leading to a restructuring of the Indian economic, social and political systems -- and the reduction of the numbers of people living in poverty.

There were others within the Congress whose beliefs were more traditional and conservative, and whose commitment to agrarian reforms was uncertain. Such men as Rajendra Prasad, later to be the first president of the Republic of India, were representative of this segment within the Congress. And it was this segment, more often than not, which held the balance of power within the policy-making echelons of the movement. Even Mahatma Gandhi, whose influence generally bridged the gap between those roughly classified as "radicals" and "conservatives", was clearly ambivalent on the question of agrarian reforms. Though deeply concerned with peasant problems and capable of winning over to the Congress a number of peasant reform movements from about 1920 in Bengal, Bihar, the United Provinces and the Punjab, Gandhi was also intimately associated with the landed elite and the large industrialists who were the principal financiers of the Congress movement. Generously interpreted, the Mahatma's behavior and message emphasized the importance of ensuring that the independence movement embraced all sorts of people, even those having divergent interests. His focus was on ensuring that landlords and industrialists, peasants and workers, would find common cause in the struggle for freedom. His message was the antithesis of class struggle. He preached the importance of mutual forbearance and tolerance. He suggested that peasants and workers, whatever their grievances, should not withhold rent or go on strikes, and that landlords and industrialists, as "trustees' of the assets in their hands, should provide good living and working conditions, take only a "just" amount in rent from tenant farmers, and pay "fair" wages to workers. A less generous interpretation of the Mahatma's behavior and message (with particular reference to agrarian reforms) would emphasize that under the application of his teaching the landlords would lose nothing and the peasants gain nothing.

Given the composition of the Congress movement, it cannot be surprising that its commitment to agrarian reforms would be highly qualified and equivocating. Such a commitment, in itself, would have had negative consequences for public policy. But, the situation worsened after independence when agrarian reforms were set aside conceptually, and not perceived as a critical strand of an integrated agricultural development strategy in which scientific and technological change would be complemented by changes in traditional institutions affecting people's rights to land. In effect, if not always in the language of the Five Year Plans, agricultural policy became dichotomized. Agrarian reforms were split-off and classified as having to do with social change, social justice, and the well-being of poor peasants. As such, while they were clearly associated with laudable goals of public policy, such reforms were perceived to be separate and distinct from the primary question facing Indian agriculture. How can the nation grow more food quickly to meet the needs of a rapidly growing population and, in the context of nationalist fervor, become self-sufficient in food production at the earliest possible date? As this question became paramount, growth-oriented agricultural programs were seen as requiring concentrated action on their own terms. In time, agricultural policy became almost exclusively growth-centered and technologically driven -- to the neglect of socioeconomic or institutional changes that might have been derived from meaningful agrarian reforms.

Agrarian Reforms Discouraged
by Foreign Aid Institutions

As growth-centered, technology-driven development policy gained credibility in India, it was encouraged by foreign aid institutions. Agrarian reforms were not similarly encouraged by such institutions, private or governmental. Foreign experts offered an approach to rural development that was production-oriented and divorced from notions of agrarian structural change: an approach, therefore, that coincided with the interests of substantial sections of India's ruling elite who clearly hoped that economic progress might be achieved somewhat painlessly in rural areas, in a fashion not threatening the dominant status of landholding elites.[25]

What follows is a brief account of the process by which "external ideas" concerning rural development came to India and, with the endorsement of indigenous elites, diverted attention from agrarian reforms.

To an unusual degree, it has been fashionable in modern India to look for answers to rural development problems in the experience of others. Although Mahatma Gandhi briefly projected a particular vision of idealized village communities in which people would act in concert to address common needs, Nehru looked beyond Indian tradition and outside of the subcontinent for inspiration and advice on how best to modernize traditional agriculture.

Within a few years of independence, India became the adopted home of scores of specialists, mostly from the United States, in rural development. Each had his own perception of what would be essential in order to promote economic development in rural India. Yet, while particular projects and rural development strategies varied over time, embedded in the various approaches suggested by foreign experts were values and assumptions associated with mainstream neoclassical economics as taught in Western institutions of higher education. It is not surprising, then, that the diverse approaches to rural development in India (including pilot projects, community development programs, intensive agricultural district programs, the creation of agricultural universities patterned after land grant institutions in the United States, and, finally, the new strategy in agriculture associated somewhat misleadingly with the phrase Green Revolution) had a common focus and therefore asked the same paramount question -- "How can we ensure more rapid increases in food production in the aggregate?"

---

25. In this context it is useful to read George Rosen's *Western Economists and Eastern Societies: Agents of Change in South Asia, 1950-1970.* (Baltimore and London: The Johns Hopkins University Press, 1985). In that work Rosen provides an account of the process by which India abandoned institutional change in the form of land reform for policies rooted in new technology.

It was assumed that any strategy effecting rapid increases in aggregate food production would ensure benefits to the mass of the people. Existing inequalities in the distribution of land and the quasi-feudal nature of the rural economy in some regions of the subcontinent were not generally perceived, if perceived at all, to be impediments to the process by which food, when produced, would in fact be distributed.[26] Besides, the food production issues seemed to be paramount and to require concerted action by public and private sector institutions. If, subsequently, there were to be distribution problems, these would be addressed automatically through "the market" after productivity increases had been achieved.

This way of thinking about India's rural development problems did not focus on the socioeconomic environments of the region (or on questions of agrarian structure). Neither did it focus on historical institutions (including land systems) that defined those environments, and would affect the process by which productivity goals and food distribution needs would be addressed. In short, the issues of rural development in India were defined increasingly at the working level in a fashion that neglected careful examination of the actual conditions affecting peoples' relationships to the land. This, in itself, should not be surprising. Those "outsiders" who helped to shape rural development strategies in the subcontinent were, for the most part, devoid of prior experience in the region. Many were specialists in agronomic research and extension services who had been trained in other environments. One of the most distinguished, whose initial exposure to India had been an accident of World War II, was trained as an architect. Through no fault of their

---

26. There was also an obvious reluctance to recognize the positive relationship between "land reforms" and the need for increases in productivity. Land reforms, when effectively implemented, are not simply a means of ensuring improved distribution of food grains; they can be conducive to increases in output because they provide new options (including what Amartya Sen calls a food entitlement) and incentives to the landless cultivators who receive secure rights to land. [See Dorner, Peter. *Land Reform and Economic Development.* (Middlesex, England: Penguin Books, 1972.)]

own, these persons were not "language and area scholars" in the field of South Asian Studies. Among the outsiders, such a "tribe" did not then exist.

With few exceptions the outsiders were not inclined to question whether local institutions (including historical land and tenure systems) might impede or facilitate the realization of their goals. As they looked for ideas and answers to India's food security and rural development needs, they drew inevitably on their own training and experience -- training and experience derived elsewhere under different historical and institutional conditions. It is no wonder then that their collective definition of modernity in agriculture, and how to achieve it, would be rooted in the theory and practice of agriculture in the United States.

It is in the context of this "external focus" on "modernity in agriculture" that successive rural development strategies have been promoted in India. Analyses and the formation of policies and programs have generally been separated from socioeconomic conditions in the region. In practice, this has meant that rural development programs contained implicit assumptions about local environments, including, for example, assumptions that farmers would be rational, profit maximizers when properly exposed to new ideas and technology and appropriately supplied with new inputs at prices ensuring favorable returns on investments. And, on those few occasions when a favorable socioeconomic environment -- including fully developed markets -- could not be assumed, steps were taken to introduce new ideas in districts, areas and states where conditions were perceived to be favorable because agricultural production increases had already therein been achieved within existing conditions.

When qualified successes in production-oriented rural development programs were accomplished, extravagant claims sometimes followed. Some referred to the prairie-fire-like spread of new technology in agriculture, and suggested that the only limitations on the spread effects of the new technology would be the nonavailability of adequate amounts of water and other physical inputs. Indeed, for some time the availability of these essential physical inputs was the only internationally recognized local condition in India that seemed critical to the success or failure of that production-oriented rural development strategy. In this fashion it became an international cliche and an accepted axiom of rural development that "local conditions" could be defined in purely technical, agronomic terms. Local conditions, by this measure, had nothing to do with the historical land systems of the subcontinent, and the hierarchy of interests in land, that would in many regions of India inhibit people's abilities to behave as independent, profit-maximizing farmers. And, the dichotomy continued to grow between the socioeconomic emphasis of agrarian reforms and the food production emphasis of applied agricultural policy.

What became known popularly in India as the "New Strategy of Agricultural Development" was acclaimed internationally before being introduced in the subcontinent. Its initial reputation was fostered by the Rockefeller and Ford Foundations (and notably in India by Rockefeller's Ralph Cummings). But the path to its adoption in India as a national program was initially uncertain. According to C. Subramaniam, who ultimately supported the new strategy from his position in the Indian cabinet as Minister for Food and Agriculture and Community Development from 1964-1967, some Indian scientists were skeptical about the need to import high-yielding varieties of wheat from far-off Mexico. They pointed out that Indian scientists had themselves been evolving new seed varieties and would continue to do so. Others in India were cynical about the dissemination of the new varieties, suggesting that the new seeds were likely to be successful in demonstration plots, but not within the framework of traditional agriculture. Similarly, there were Indian economists who worried about the long-term costs of introducing seed varieties so dependent on large quantities of fertilizer -- especially given the likelihood that the strategy would require the government to use scarce foreign exchange to import needed fertilizer. A few pointed out that, with the failure to implement meaningful land reforms in much of India, it seemed likely that farmers with large holdings (well-established traditional landholders) would have greater access to the new seeds and other inputs than would less powerful farmers, usually small landholders. In such circumstances, they argued, the strategy would be associated with widening income inequalities in the countryside, and rural tensions would be a derivative of the introduction of the new technology. Meanwhile, the communist group in Parliament had its own perspective. It associated the new strategy with increasing dependence on the United States and expressed the fear that the country would be vulnerable to U.S. exploitation.

Subramaniam pressed for the adoption of the new strategy, especially at a time when India was importing annually more than ten million metric tons of food grains. He argued that it would be better to import fertilizer from the West, in an attempt to become self-sufficient in the production of basic foodstuffs, than to remain dependent on food imports from the United States. In due course, the internal climate turned in favor of the new strategy and steps were taken to implement it.

"Green Revolution" became the internationally accepted term used to describe the process by which high-yielding varieties of cereals (supported by intensive use of chemical fertilizers in controlled quantities, insecticides, pesticides and regulated water supplies) would be disseminated in many regions of India in the 1970s. The rapid spread effects of this package of inputs in some regions (notably in the Punjab, Haryana and western Uttar Pradesh) created enormous expectations for continuing aggregate production increases (especially of wheat).

Later, Green Revolution successes were expressed in qualified terms. Wheat was correctly perceived as the crop that benefitted most from the new technology. It was noted, however, that while wheat production was trebling, rice production rose only by some 16 percent. And, even Green Revolution enthusiasts accepted the notion that there were, at least, some critical physical constraints to the spread of the new technology. The diffusion of high-yielding varieties of rice was less rapid in areas prone to waterlogging and deep flooding -- representing 80 percent of the rice growing areas of India.

But, even if the new technology would not spread as rapidly as a prairie-fire, or be equally applicable to all cereals, there was comfort in the impression that the only constraints on its dissemination could be discussed in technocratic, physical terms. If water was a primary constraint, dams could be constructed, channels deepened and tube wells dug. These were engineering problems --

easy to conceptualize and address in physical terms. Moreover, such problems could be examined in a fashion that need not take into account the socioeconomic conditions in some regions of India that would ultimately limit some cultivators' access to water -- even when irrigation systems were put in place.

The pendulum swung gradually from enthusiasm for the productivity effects of the new technology to qualification concerning the strategy's appropriateness in some regions and, finally, to concern that the technology would be associated with widening income inequality. Some asked, could there be rapid growth plus equity? Even if a production-oriented strategy of rural development seemed to be consistent with the interests of those who ruled, could such a strategy be reconciled with the long-term rhetorical commitment to distributive justice?

In the 1980s, there seems to be an international consensus that peasant cultivators with secure rights in land have gained relative to tenants and laborers from the adoption of the higher yielding grain varieties. Although it can be argued that marginal farmers with insecure rights in land -- together with tenants, sharecroppers, and wage laborers -- have often received some benefits from increases in aggregate production, there is also evidence (regionally differentiated in India) of a widening absolute gap in income distribution between landowners and those having insecure rights in land or no land at all. Nevertheless, if there is any continuing debate in contemporary India concerning the income distribution effects of the nation's production-oriented agricultural development policy, it seems to be carried out in muted tones.

There is no need here to establish a final judgment on the effects in India of the strategy dominated by new technology in agriculture. Even critics must admit that the new technology's productive effects have been important, if regionally differentiated. Moreover, it should be noted that the rudiments of the approach are neither inherently good nor bad. What must increasingly be understood is that, when the new technology is introduced in regions of great inequality in the distribution of rights in land, the spread effects of the new technology will be limited and will be distributed in a fashion that reflects and reinforces existing inequalities. In other words, though applied policy may separate technological inputs from agrarian reforms, the implementation of technological approaches to rural development is both affected by and affects the existing hierarchy of interests in land. When technology is introduced without regard to the existing agrarian structure, it cannot help but contribute to the exacerbation of problems already deeply embedded in the socioeconomic structures of rural India.

Agrarian Reforms Linked to Agrarian Relations

Growth of Agrarian Unrest. In the early 1950s, the traditional structure of relationships of men to the land in India seemed immutable. In many regions of the country, and particularly in the Eastern region defined by the Permanent Settlement of 1793, power was concentrated in the hands of landholders, particularly those classified under law as *zamindars* and tenure-holders. It was my observation then that the rural poor[27] had neither the capacity nor the vision required to challenge those above them in the rural hierarchy. Landless laborers, sharecroppers, and small farmers could not then conceptualize a process of social and economic change that would affect them positively.

The years since the 1950s have been ones in which various programs initiated by government -- even programs judged to be failures -- have altered the traditional system of relationships among rural haves and have-nots in many regions of India. Forty years of government interventions in rural India, and the worsening of the man-to-land ratio in the countryside as a derivative of the doubling of

27. I am using the term rural poor here not to specify persons having low levels of income, but rather those having low status in the agrarian hierarchy either because they have tenuous rights in land or no land at all. I am using the term in a fashion that I consider to be consistent with Amartya Sen's concern about poverty and entitlements -- the focus emphasizing legal rights, or the absence of them, that affect peoples' ability to fulfill basic needs. [See Sen's *Poverty and Famines: An Essay on Entitlement and Deprivation.* (Oxford: Clarendon Press, 1981), Chapter 10.]

India's population in the same period, have made plain to increasing numbers of the peasantry that traditional agrarian systems and the relationships shaped by them are not immutable. Government initiated agrarian reforms -- even when drafted consciously to minimize change in traditional, hierarchical relationships in the countryside -- have produced direct and indirect changes in agrarian structures, contributed to disputes over rights in land, and have fueled tensions between those having secure rights in land and those who, while dependent on agriculture for survival, do not. Attempts by government to introduce new technology in agriculture, to initiate major and minor irrigation works, to improve the availability of rural credit, to promote rural electrification, and to extend the coverage of mass communication systems to the countryside have gradually transformed old patterns of interaction between established authority and the peasantry, and have spread awareness in the countryside that change in the traditional order is inevitable -- and in many instances desirable.

Today an indeterminate but clearly growing number of India's peasantry embrace the notion that change in their traditional mode of life is both desirable and possible. And, the notion that change is possible has been endorsed and cultivated, at least periodically, by politicians of all persuasions, by government officials performing new functions in rural areas, and by the "messages" conveyed as systems of mass communication increasingly penetrated the countryside.

It has been evident now for at least twenty years that the rural masses would no longer deliver votes automatically. The ruling elite began to get that message during the general elections of 1967 when the traditional dominance of the Congress Party was first shattered, and it was widely perceived that an era had dawned in which the support of rural voters could not be taken for granted. In the period following the elections, there were widespread incidents of agrarian unrest. Roving bands of peasants forcibly harvested the standing crops of landlords in Purnea, Bhagalpur, and Darbhanga districts of Bihar. And, in 1968, peasants of Champaran district encroached on government lands, and landless laborers demanded land from government officials in the districts of Bhagalpur,

Monghyr, Gaya and Chapra. Meanwhile in West Bengal, there were frequent and violent outbreaks of agrarian unrest in the region of Naxalbari and elsewhere in the state. By August of 1969, 346 separate incidents of forcible occupation of land had been reported from West Bengal, and similar incidents occurring with increasing frequency were reported not only in Bihar and West Bengal, but also in Assam, Andhra Pradesh, Gujarat, Kerala, Orissa, Punjab, Rajasthan, Tamil Nadu, and Uttar Pradesh.[28]

For several years thereafter, the central government showed heightened awareness and concern about agrarian unrest in India. A unit within the Home Ministry associated this unrest with the persistence of serious social and economic inequalities and the failure of various programs, including agrarian reforms, to meet the needs of the rural poor. The Ministry argued that a continuing failure to meet such needs would leave the field to "certain political parties,"[29] who had already demonstrated some success in various regions to organize dissident groups of peasants by appealing to their hunger for land and their awakened interest in improved standards of living. The Ministry stated that after twenty-two years of planned rural development the traditional landholders remained powerful and "... the programmes so far implemented are still more favorable to the larger owner-farmer than to the smaller tenant-farmer. As for the sharecropper and the landless labourer, they have been more often than not left out in the cold. In consequence ... disparities have widened, accentuating social tensions ..." and producing

---

28. "The Causes and Nature of Current Agrarian Tensions." Annexure I. (New Delhi: Government of India, Ministry of Home Affairs, 1969).

29. It seemed evident at the time that the oblique reference of the Home Ministry was to the Communist Party of India (Marxist) and the Communist Party of India (Marxist-Leninist). These parties were then considered capable of exploiting existing tensions in rural areas (especially in pockets of eastern India) -- tensions produced, according to the Home Ministry, by a widening economic gap between the relatively few affluent farmers and the large body of small landholders and landless agricultural workers.

problems, concluded the Ministry, requiring urgent action by appropriate authorities.

Following selective dissemination of the Home Ministry's 1969 report, Prime Minister Indira Gandhi called for a new agricultural development strategy which would require, in her words, not only organization and inputs but also the removal of existing institutional and social impediments to production. Among measures to forestall further growth of agrarian tensions, she specifically insisted that ceilings on the size of landholdings be implemented on a priority basis so that surplus land could be distributed to the landless. In a fashion that would be repeated in the years ahead, the central government urged the states to fulfill earlier promises to transform traditional agrarian structures through speedy, efficient and effective programs of agrarian reforms. Even after the declaration of the state of emergency in India in 1975, and later still, government chose to reiterate old themes packaged in twenty-point programs of economic and agrarian reforms -- reforms that seemed periodically to suggest that the ruling elite might yet recognize that the maintenance of its power and legitimacy would ultimately require the implementation of economic programs which addressed the needs of have-not communities in rural areas.

In other words, the agrarian reform themes consistently reiterated at the Centre suggest that at least some of the ruling elite recognize the need to perceive the rural "have-nots" not only as potential threats to the stability of the Indian political system, but also as potential sources of political support, if such "have-nots" can be addressed and mobilized by a group capable of interpreting and meeting their needs. Unfortunately, the reiteration of plans and promises, when not followed by effective implementation of reforms, serves in the long run to exacerbate rural tensions, rather than to engender social stability and political support. And, agrarian reforms, as verbalized, enacted, and implemented can be said in this context to have contributed to a further separation of the rural poor from the ruling elites, rather than to a unification of the interests of both groups.

Effects of Agrarian Reforms. Agrarian reforms have clearly failed as "land reform." If one dares to generalize on this theme, it can be said that the complex body of land reform legislation as enacted and implemented in India has not conferred land to the tiller.[30] In the general case, few peasant cultivators at the base of the agrarian hierarchy (particularly sharecroppers and landless agricultural laborers) have received secure rights in land as a consequence of reform legislation. Even legislation designed to put a ceiling on the size of landholdings has not led to the acquisition and distribution of sufficient land declared "surplus" even to begin to address the persistent hunger for land in rural India. And, coincident with the enactment of agrarian reforms legislation, there has been clear evidence that the number of landless households in rural India has been growing, as has the percentage of the landless to the rural population as a whole.

The growth in the number of landless households in rural India can be attributed to an uncertain degree to a country-wide process by which peasant cultivators, lacking adequate documentation of their rights in land, have been evicted from lands customarily tilled by them by landholders enjoying "superior" rights in land. The growth in landless households who remain tied to agriculture must also be attributed, of course, to the doubling of India's population in the last thirty-five years and the slow growth of non-agricultural employment opportunities for the landless.

In short, land reform has failed widely to confer "land to the tiller;" it has failed as a means of providing land for the landless; it is associated with the growth in the number of landless households in rural areas who remain dependent on agriculture for employment; and, it is associated with the growth of litigation over rights in land.

Yet, these "failed reforms" have had a profound and continuously evolving effect on agrarian relations in rural India. These failed reforms have contributed to the destruction of the old equilibrium of the countryside, represented by the reciprocal obligations of patron and

---

30. In this context, see, for example, Ronald Herring's *Land to the Tiller: The Political Economy of Agrarian Reform in South Asia* (New Haven: Yale University Press, 1983).

client, landlord and peasant farmer. Having weakened the nexus between those having superior and inferior rights to land, the effects of "failed reforms" can be said to have included providing the basis for the emergence of new standards of behavior, and for conflict between the traditional elites and the marginal people in the countryside who were, in some instances, partial beneficiaries of reforms or non-beneficiaries of failed programs. As my colleague, Ronald Herring, has observed: "The structural change which is seldom analyzed by scholars of land reform is at the ideational level." New attitudes, expectations, and fears have permeated the countryside of India as peculiar derivatives of failed programs. As Herring has suggested, land reforms have prompted the organization of landed interests where none had previously existed; the landless have (in regionally differentiated ways) been mobilized and organized to demand the enforcement of tenancy legislation, or the redistribution of land perceived by them to be surplus.[31]

Clearly, agrarian reforms have not resolved the problem of rural poverty in India. But, even reforms classified as failures have contributed to rural peoples' ideas concerning the legitimacy and possibility of change in the conditions that affect them. In many regions of India today, new coalitions are being formed to challenge the political and economic power of the traditional, landholding elites. The essence of the challenge centers on the control of scarce land resources in a society that remains predominantly agrarian. It is by no means certain, in the near term, that those who challenge the landholding elites will succeed in overthrowing them. What does seem certain is that the tension and conflict among traditional and emerging groups will in time produce change in the political economy of the nation.

What is also evident is that there is no escaping the dilemma posed by the prospects of continuing social, economic, and political change in a climate of group conflict and tension. There is no turning back to a rural society in seeming equilibrium -- where intermediaries (landlords), cultivating peasants having secure rights to

---

31. Ibid., pp. 270-271.

land (*raiyats*), peasant farmers having tenuous rights to
land (*under-raiyats*), sharecroppers, and landless laborers
interact within structures imposed and reinforced by
tradition.[32] Those at the bottom of India's agrarian
hierarchy -- roughly categorized here as the rural poor
because they lack either secure rights to land or any land
at all -- are less subservient to authority in 1988 than
they were forty-one years ago. With each election, their
votes are less easily mobilized and procured. These people
can no longer be described as stolid and stunned, brothers
to the bullocks in the fields. Instead, they are now
capable of placing demands -- often backed by militant
action -- on India's economic and political systems. If the
ruling elites fail to respond to the legitimate interests of
sections of the peasantry who constitute the rural poor,
they risk in the long run losing the opportunity to preside
over and influence a process of orderly social, economic
and political change -- thus leaving the field to those who
believe in the legitimacy of violence, on the one hand
those who would act violently to promote change and on
the other those who would act violently to forestall it.

A Contemporary Agenda for Action

Targeting the Eastern Region of India. There is a
recognized need in contemporary India to increase
agricultural productivity in the eastern region comprising
West Bengal, Orissa, Bihar and eastern Uttar Pradesh. This
region, with land and water resources that are inherently
richer than those of the Punjab, Haryana and western
Uttar Pradesh, has not begun to realize its productive
potential; its productive achievements in agriculture have
been well below attainable levels.[33]

---

32. The terms *raiyats* and *under-raiyats* are used here to refer loosely to
general categories of peasant cultivators in an all-India context. The terms
are, in a *de jure* sense, regionally specific within India, rather than universal
in application.

33. For elaboration on this theme from an "official" perspective, see, for
(continued...)

To encourage economic progress in the region, the Government of India seems to have embraced a development strategy that is once again unidimensional -- based almost exclusively on the new technology in agriculture. For example, the Reserve Bank of India's two volume report entitled *Agricultural Productivity in Eastern India* recommends a development strategy emphasizing the massive provision of tube wells and pump sets, the improvement of drainage and water management techniques, research and extension, the creation of energy resources, custom services and post harvest arrangements for the storage and marketing of crops. It suggests assisting small and marginal farmers through science-based and industry-linked farming technology. It urges the promotion of high yielding varieties of crops through the adoption of what it refers to as "labor-cum-capital" intensive techniques.

There is little recognition in the report that the agrarian structure of the region may itself constitute an impediment to economic progress. This notwithstanding, the report does present credible data, for example, on the distribution of rights in land in Bihar (the state having the greatest potential for increases in agricultural production in the region, and probably in India as a whole). It even recognizes the persistence of absentee landlordism in that state, notes that sharecropping is widespread, and that (though tenancy is legally prohibited in Bihar) it is estimated that about one-third of the land is held (and tilled) under oral lease arrangements.[34] Having also established that operational holdings in Bihar are both small and fragmented, the report goes on to urge (as does the Seventh Five Year Plan) what I consider to be the least meaningful of agrarian reforms for Bihar and the eastern region: the idea that existing landholdings should be consolidated in order to provide an improved

---

33(...continued)
example, the Reserve Bank of India's two volume report entitled *Agricultural Productivity in Eastern India*, (Bombay: 1984).

34. *Agricultural Productivity in Eastern India.* (Bombay: Reserve Bank of India, 1984), pp. 236-237.

environment for government's "Special Programme for Rice Production" (to be effected in the Seventh Plan).[35]

What is clearly being ignored as government contemplates how best it can encourage increased productivity in the eastern region of India is the appropriateness of a synthetic strategy of agricultural development -- a strategy that recognizes that the environment for the diffusion of new technology in agriculture would be enhanced if simultaneous efforts were made not only to disseminate new technology but also to provide security of tenure to the actual tillers of the region -- those small farmers and sharecroppers whose rights to land are either tenuous or non-existent (but who, nonetheless, till in Bihar alone at least 42 percent of the cultivated area). It should be obvious, as never before with respect to this region, that new technology in agriculture is a necessary, but not sufficient condition, for economic progress. Moreover, in a region where agrarian unrest has been evident for decades, it should also be apparent to the ruling elite that agrarian reforms -- even of the tenurial sort -- would have political as well as

35. The proponents of "consolidation of holdings" are clearly interested in reducing the number of small holdings and encouraging economies of scale in agricultural production. Those who press for consolidation of holdings generally ignore cultivators' rational reasons for having fragmented holdings: to diversify their cropping patterns and to provide a hedge against the possible failure of an entire crop planted in a single block in one area. That is to say, the division of a small holding into several non-contiguous plots may serve the economie interests of a "security maximizing" cultivator. For such a cultivator, each plot has a different purpose within the framework of an agricultural year. One low lying plot catches a greater share than others of the Summer monsoon and helps to ensure the subsequent harvest; another plot on higher ground ensures a Spring return on a crop which might otherwise suffer from the effects of too much standing water following the monsoon. Thus, consolidation of holdings, as an agrarian reform, is no panacea for increasing agricultural production. The merits of such a reform must be evaluated in a particular context. As suggested in the text above, such a reform is the "least meaningful" of possible agrarian reforms in the eastern region of India because it tends to be fostered within a vision of economic progress (rooted in a particular, economic ideology) that abstracts from actual cultivators' needs and interests, as I see them, in that region.

economic significance. Surely this last point is made evident by the political returns of "Operation Barga" to the Government of West Bengal in 1987, as detailed earlier in this essay.

Employing the Residual Powers of the Centre. If a synthetic strategy for rural development could be articulated for the eastern region (one that ended the dichotomy in agricultural development programs between technology and agrarian reforms) the central government of India could use its residual powers as "super-landlord" to ensure[36] that the necessary agrarian reforms were put into effect. The background and rationale for this proposition are outlined in the following paragraphs.[37]

Contravening nationalist sentiment in India, Daniel Thorner long ago suggested that the British did not introduce private property in land into India. The key feature of the British land settlements of the late eighteenth and nineteenth centuries, whether *zamindari*, *raiyatwari*, *mahalwari*, *taluqdari*, or *malguzari*, whether permanent or temporary, was that the rights in land recognized by the British were invariably subordinate to those of the state. "To no holder was granted the exclusive right to occupy, enjoy and dispose of land which, in practice," said Thorner, "is the hallmark of Western private ownership."[38] While some of the rights normally associated with private property in land (transfer,

---

36. I recognize here, of course, that the strategy, by itself, could not "ensure" that agrarian reforms were put into effect. The strategy assumes that the central government would have the political will to enforce its behavior as "super-landlord." I would be the first to accept the notion that this is a large assumption -- and possibly an unwarranted one within the political economy of contemporary India.

37. While the following section focuses on a rural development strategy said to be applicable to the eastern region, the strategy, in its essence, could have all-India implications. If effected by the Centre, the strategy would enhance the powers of the central government in dealing with seemingly intractable agrarian structural questions in various regions of the country.

38. Thorner, Daniel. *The Agrarian Prospect in India.* (Delhi: University Press, 1956), p. 7.

mortgageability, and heritability) were accorded by the British to those with whom they made their settlements, it was made plain within the context of those settlements that others simultaneously held superior and inferior rights pertaining to the same lands. That is to say, the State, or governing authority, continued to claim a share of the rents in the form of land revenue, while actual tillers continued to exercise continuing claims of "occupancy."

As the British established territorial control in India, they established their supreme rights in land; as super-landlords they continued to collect land revenue (the state's share of the produce).

What is striking about the agrarian structure of India, forty-one years after the British Raj was ended, is that a key element in the traditional agrarian structure persists. That is to say, the states' claims to land, and ultimately the central government's claims to land, remain supreme. The Indian states continue to collect land revenue. All claimants to land below the state have, to varying degrees, "inferior" rights in land. And, notwithstanding the enacted legislation for agrarian reforms, I believe that it can be said that the great body of laws, regulations and rules brought into being by the British to enforce property relations and to collect the states' revenues from the land remain intact.

Given this peculiar history of property rights in land, India's central government could exert its authority as the "supreme landlord" to effect necessary changes in the status of tillers of the soil in the eastern region, as well as in other regions of India. Such action on the part of the central government of India would be consistent with long established traditions dating to the nineteenth century when the British effort was to protect actual tillers or "tenants" from eviction by landlords by establishing rules and procedures by which tenants could establish what were called then "permanent occupancy rights" to lands tilled by them. Operation Barga in contemporary West Bengal, as mentioned earlier is clearly derived as much from that nineteenth century tradition as from any modern motivation.

What now is needed is the political will among the ruling elite to ensure the future by rediscovering a means of action endorsed by past practice.[39]   What now is needed is the recognition that agrarian reforms may yet have both economic and political saliency in the arena of public policy -- particularly in the eastern region of the country where the concern must be to foster rural development which contributes not only to increases in production, but also to improved participation in economic progress among segments of the rural poor (defined by their present tenuous legal and *de facto* rights in land).

In sum, in the days ahead, the persistent issue in the agrarian sector (not only in eastern India, but in the country as a whole) confronting those who would lead India will no longer be "How can we grow more food?" The country already has production-oriented, technology-driven answers to that old question -- answers that are troubling because they confirm that the approach which has been emphasized is associated nationally with growing regional inequalities together with growing inequalities among people within regions.   In these circumstances, the persistent concern at the Centre must be focused not only on how best to maintain aggregate growth rates in the agrarian sector, but also on how to ensure that the benefits of growth are in fact distributed in a fashion likely to promote the general welfare and to contribute broadly to peoples' sense of full participation in India's political economy.   From this perspective, the new question in India must be "Who is producing on whose land for whose benefit?"   Such a question would give no less attention to production issues, but would at the same time make plain the importance of poverty alleviation.   Such a question would revive and give renewed emphasis to the maintenance of India's old commitment to the establishment of a more egalitarian, democratic society within which economic progress is defined in holistic terms.

---

39. For those who would question utilizing within independent India means developed in the past by British colonialists, I would say only that the Government of India, after independence, has repeatedly maintained systematically most of the rules and procedures of governance inherited from the colonial period.

4

THE ARENA OF
NATIONAL SECURITY

EXTERNAL THREATS TO SECURITY

India is not only the dominant power in the South Asia region, but also faces no immediate threat from its neighbors -- although one cannot ignore persistent tensions with Pakistan and the fact that the border disputes with the People's Republic of China are still, as it were, "on the table." China still claims substantial areas bordering Tibet in the eastern Himalayas, and India the 36,000 square mile area of Aksai Chin in the western Himalayas.[1] And,

---

1. Though China withdrew from territory in the eastern border region that it had earlier disputed and briefly occupied in the Sino-Indian border war of 1962, it still claims roughly 56,000 square miles of territory in the eastern zone of the subcontinent. Following the failure of the seventh round of talks on the Sino-Indian border in Beijing in July of 1986, the unilateral decision of the Government of India on February 20, 1987, to include disputed territory in its new, northeastern state of Arunachal once again heightened tension between India and China in that region. Beijing described the Indian move "... as an act which grossly violated China's sovereignty and territorial integrity." [Far Eastern Economic Review, (March 5, 1987), p.8] There were subsequent reports [e.g., an article by Lena H. Sun entitled "Talks to Air Sino-Indian Tension: Armies Said Poised on Contested Border" in The Washington Post, (June 15, 1987), p. 16.] of increased military activity in the region, and it was estimated that India had at least 11 divisions, including para-military forces, in the northeastern border areas facing similarly large Chinese units. It seemed evident in June of 1987 that border skirmishes between Chinese and Indian troops could result from actions already taken by

(continued...)

though Pakistan might like to challenge India's hegemony in the region, Pakistan is in no position to do so -- even though it is difficult for Indian leaders to accept the notion that Pakistan is, in comparison with India, a weak and vulnerable state.

From the perspective of outsiders who claim some knowledge of South Asia, India's seeming preoccupation with the threat posed by Pakistan to its security seems, variously, either to be irrational or a calculated means of defending its own military build-up. To suggest that India does not enjoy a favorable military balance with Pakistan (because, for example, India must maintain forces along the Himalayan frontiers and, therefore, the number of combat divisions that can be fielded on the Indo-Pakistan border by both sides is said to be about the same), is to engage in tactical obfuscation concerning the relative strengths of the two sides.[2] Nonetheless, we must anticipate that India will continue officially to perceive Pakistan as a major external threat to its national security. This holds especially so long as the United States provides substantial flows of economic and military assistance to Pakistan.

Moreover, it is apparent that India has accepted the Great Power notion that "national security" is a commodity best purchased with increasingly sophisticated weapons --

---

1(...continued)

both sides. It also seemed unlikely, however, that India and China would allow border tensions to deteriorate into a war that neither nation wanted or could afford. Yet, as long as the border between China and India remains largely undemarcated and in dispute, and diplomatic talks are stalled, there is the obvious possibility that miscalculations on both sides could lead to fighting at strategic points along the Sino-Indian frontier. What might happen then, nobody knows. While "... both these great Asian powers would probably intend initially to keep their hostilities localized and finite ... all the factors would be present to work towards spreading the fighting and extending it in duration in a classic case of escalation." [For elaboration on this last theme, see Néville Maxwell's article entitled "Towards India's Second China War?" in *South*, (May, 1987).]

2. In this context, see, for example, the discussion of the "military balance" between India and Pakistan in *India Today*, Volume X Number 21, (November 15, 1985).

weapons frequently justified by suppliers and purchasers as
providing security against external threats. Indeed, both
Pakistan and India are locked in an arms race that
virtually mirrors that of the United States and the Soviet
Union. While no nation can choose to ignore potential
threats that may indeed have some external dimensions,
what is clearly needed in India is the courage to question
whether national security can be achieved by military
expenditures alone, and whether supposed external threats
to national security loom larger in the days ahead than
internal threats. Is the threat of Pakistan to India, when
examined without passion or paranoia, sufficiently real and
substantive to justify utilizing increasing quantities of
scarce resources for military hardware -- resources that
might otherwise be used for development purposes to add
meaningfully to the numbers of Indians who have a stake
in economic progress, and possibly even enhanced
commitment to the Indian political system? I doubt it.
Whatever the nature of external threats to India, I believe
that the nation's security and long-term viability will rest
on whether the diverse peoples of India are given tangible
grounds for belief that their political economic system
functions well enough to provide food, clothing, shelter,
and expanding opportunities for a decent life to ever
widening numbers of citizens. From this perspective, the
most obvious threat to India's national security is internal,
and is taking shape now when literally hundreds of millions
of people are essentially non-participants in economic
progress, yet cognizant in increasing numbers of the
promises of better days to come made to them repeatedly
for forty-one years by the governing elites, especially when
seeking votes at the time of elections. The time is past
ripe in India for a new and broadened definition of
national security that makes plain that in the days ahead
internal threats can be potentially more severe and
destabilizing than external threats.[3]

---

3. Jagat S. Mehta, former Foreign Secretary to the Government of India, is
among those who have persistently argued that Third World nations (and
notably India and Pakistan) should not permit their security interests to be
focused almost exclusively on external threats -- particularly threats defined
(continued...)

It is by no means probable, however, that India's leaders, including Rajiv Gandhi, will refine their definition of national security to give additional, appropriate emphasis to "internal threats," and work to establish, therefore, a long-term *modus vivendi* with Pakistan (not to mention a settlement of border issues with China).[4] The trend is in another direction. The historical distrust and antipathy for Pakistan in India is deeply embedded. It is fueled by the memories of three wars between Pakistan and India (1947, 1965, and 1971). It is associated with communalism: the sense among many Hindus in India that Muslims, particularly in Pakistan, remain the ancient enemy. It is reinforced by events that buffet the region. The Soviet intervention in Afghanistan and the American response have given new strength to those forces in India (and in Pakistan) who define national security myopically in terms of military hardware, and seek to acquire the latest technology from the superpowers, their surrogates, or others. And, the distrust and antipathy expressed by India and Pakistan for each other will not now be diminished easily when Pakistan seems to have developed nuclear weapons capability, and is intent on acquiring from others, or developing internally, appropriate "delivery systems" for those weapons.[5] And, notwithstanding official statements

---

3(...continued)
within the framework of great power rivalry. [For amplification on this and other relevant themes, see *Third World Militarization: A Challenge to Third World Diplomacy*, edited by Jagat S. Mehta, and published by The Lyndon B. Johnson School of Public Affairs, The University of Texas at Austin, (1985).]

4. It seems evident that India had within its grasp a border settlement with China shortly after Rajiv Gandhi took office. The opportunity for such a settlement, if it did indeed exist, may have been dissipated (in a fashion that seems inexplicable) by the decision of the Government of India in 1987 to confer statehood on Arunachal Pradesh.

5. Pakistan "virtually" announced that it had nuclear weapons capability, if not a "tested" bomb, on March 1, 1987. While there were subsequent attempts to step back from the announcement by Dr. Abdul Qader Khan, the head of Pakistan's nuclear establishment, it must be assumed that he was sending a

(continued...)

that India has "... no intention of making a nuclear bomb now,"[6] it is obvious that the arms race between Pakistan and India has entered a new and extremely costly phase.[7] What is more, it seems unlikely that the superpowers will conduct themselves in a fashion that constrains the arms race on the subcontinent. The United States seems unwilling (or unable) to restrain Pakistan. The Reagan administration has made plain that it will continue military aid to Pakistan (if unchecked by Congress) even if Pakistan pursues a nuclear weapons program. That administration's concern for nuclear non-proliferation has been outweighed by its need to use Pakistan to confront the Soviets in Afghanistan. Meanwhile, there is no evidence to suggest that the Soviet Union is in a position formally to restrain India. Moreover, India has persistently refused to consider declaring South Asia a nuclear free zone. The point of "no return" with respect to nuclear weapons programs has now

---

5(...continued)

signal to India and the world that Pakistan had joined the nuclear weapons club. Of course, it had been obvious for years that Pakistan's nuclear research and development efforts were inconsistent with a purely peaceful program. The United States Ambassador to Pakistan, Dean Hinton, said as much on February 16, 1987, in Islamabad while addressing the Pakistan Institute of Strategic Studies. India, of course, had already demonstrated its own nuclear weapons "potential" in 1974 by means of an underground nuclear blast at Pokhran in Rajasthan.

6. The quotation is from a statement made by the Minister of State for External Affairs in India's Rajya Sabha on March 13, 1987, as reported in the article "Their Bomb, Our Bomb" in the *Economic and Political Weekly*, Vol. XXII, No.12, (March 21, 1987), p. 475.

7. In his book, *Nuclear Weapons -- Policy Options for India*, Bhabani Sengupta puts the cost for India of a second generation nuclear deterrent at Rs. 15,000 crore. Furthermore, Sengupta suggests that "The cost of conventional defence cannot remain at the current level if Pakistan goes nuclear. The armed forces will, if nothing else, have to be equipped to fight a nuclear war. That means that all the western front divisions will have to be mechanized, and that alone would cost Rs. 10,000 crore over 10 years." [From "Pakistan's Nuclear Bombshell" by Dilip Bobb and Ramindar Singh in *India Today*, (March 31, 1987), p. 16.]

been passed in both India and Pakistan; there can be no
return to the *status quo ante* -- even if outsiders,
including the superpowers, have second thoughts on the
significance of what already has transpired.

INTERNAL THREATS TO SECURITY

If internal threats to India's security were given
primacy over external threats -- especially those that are
defined in accordance with the perceptions of the Soviets
or the Americans, India would find no greater threat than
that derived from regional disparities in economic growth
among the states that comprise the Republic. As
elemental documentation for this thesis,[8] we would point to
the breakup of Pakistan in 1971-1972, just three years
after Pakistan had been declared an international economic
success story by the government of the United States.
Pakistan's success had been measured in terms of aggregate
growth rates over a ten year period from 1958 to 1968; but
these aggregate measures disguised the disparities in
growth and in other indices of development between West
and East Pakistan. In the end, the principal threat to the
existence of a united Pakistan was not external (in the
form of international Communism or the policies of
neighboring states), but internal, in the form of Pakistan's
inability to see how its American-endorsed development
strategy was producing high growth rates in Pakistan's
Punjab financed, in a sense, by the impoverishment of East
Bengal (i.e., East Pakistan).

If, then, the highest-order threat to national security
in India comes ultimately from regional disparities in
economic progress in a plural society, and from peoples'
sense of being non-participants in economic progress, a
number of internal threats become obvious and can be
anticipated: for example, (1) the disparity in the rate of

---

8. I am not choosing here to lengthen this essay by elaborating the thesis
that India's national security is threatened by regional disparities in
economic growth. While the argument could benefit from elaboration, I have
chosen to support my thesis by drawing on analogous evidence from the
historical experience of India's sister state in the subcontinent, Pakistan.

growth between states in western India (e.g., Gujarat and Maharashtra) and those in the East (notably Bihar and West Bengal); and (2) the disparities in income and opportunity -- perceived and real -- between sections of the peasantry in varying regions of India who have secure rights in land and those who do not.

These internal threats to security are, in a sense, the natural and inevitable concomitants of a process whereby economic progress becomes institutionalized in India. Most economists would accept the notion that such a process will be associated, initially, with widening income inequality among regions and among groups within regions. This holds especially when the process is initiated in a plural, inegalitarian, hierarchical society. In such a society, the benefits of economic progress will be conferred unevenly -- even when attempts are made through central planning to ensure that resource flows are directed toward the least developed regions and the poorest sections of the people. That is to say, the more progressive states (with a tradition of effective public administration, with historical land systems that have not conferred contemporary conditions inimical to economic progress, with industry and social overhead capital in place, with excellent educational institutions already operating, etc.) will be expected to absorb resources effectively and to institutionalize economic progress more readily than states which lack virtually all of those assets (or initial advantages) at the outset. In the same fashion, what distinguishes the "progressive" farmer in India from the backward and poor one is that the progressive farmer begins his quest for economic advance with a secure right to land. When he receives subsidized inputs, his "progressivity" is confirmed by his effective utilization of those inputs. The backward farmer, lacking command over land, does not receive, and cannot utilize directly, the same inputs. He therefore remains backward -- which confirms in the popular mind his "backwardness."

Widening income inequality among regions and among peoples within regions poses no immediate or certain threat to internal security -- particularly in a compartmented, plural society. The internal threat comes only after some lapse of time when, for example, with the growth of regional inequalities, regional elites (possibly, e.g., in

Bombay or greater Maharashtra) take umbrage at a central government led process by which their state is taxed to support "backward" states like Bihar. In other words, the internal threat in this illustration comes when components of a plural society cease believing that the ties that bind them together are greater than the disparities (in language and culture and economic progress) that separate them. Similarly, widening income inequality among peoples within regions poses no immediate threat to internal security -- even in a hierarchical, inegalitarian agrarian society -- if the people accept their places in that hierarchy and do not challenge the power and prerogatives of those above them. In such circumstances, the threat to internal security comes only when sharecroppers and landless laborers, for whatever reasons, no longer accept the traditional hierarchy of interests and take steps to challenge the authority and prerogatives of those above them.

Having outlined above two scenarios by which threats to internal security can evolve, I would add here only that the first threat (that of growing regional disparities in economic progress among the states of India and the tensions that evolve as an outgrowth of those disparities) is acted out in the arena of Centre-state relations, and helps to explain the "tug of war" that has been institutionalized in India between the Centre and the states. The second threat to internal security (derived mainly from the long-term effects of disparities in economic progress among sections of the peasantry) is increasingly being acted out in direct conflict between competing groups. And, it is this competition (popularly portrayed in the media in caste and communal terms that disguise the economic roots of much of the conflict) that increasingly tests the mettle of and overloads local civil authorities. When thus overloaded, those authorities, in concert with the Government of India, have increasingly resorted to the use of the Indian military to restore law and order. In this fashion, the "internal threat" posed by agrarian unrest (or other kinds of disturbances) in some localities is transposed into another kind of internal threat -- one involving the potential breakdown of constitutional, civilian-led government and its eventual replacement by a new system of governance dominated by the military.

THE ROLE OF THE MILITARY

The Use of Force Against Peasant Insurgents

It has been evident for some time now that the civil authority in India has been prone to use the full range of its coercive power to repress peasant movements, particularly those said to be committed to the transformation of India by means of violent, insurrection-like activities. The quick repression in 1967 of the Naxalite uprising, led by an Indian subset of avowed Marxist-Leninists, was followed by a rapid build-up of police and para-military power in India. From 1969 to 1974, when the activities of the Communist Party of India (Marxist-Leninist) were most conspicuous in West Bengal, Bihar, Punjab, and Andhra, and while the civil police forces in all of the Indian states grew by more than 17 percent, the "armed police" grew by more than 27 percent. Meanwhile, the central government continued to invest in the development of a variety of para-military units -- for example, the Border Security Force, the Central Reserve Police Force, the Eastern Frontier Rifles, and the Central Industrial Security Force.[9] The Central Reserve Police Force, which had only sixteen battalions in 1964-1965, had sixty by 1972-1973.[10] Meanwhile, the Border Security Force was also expanded and, notwithstanding its name, used "... for maintaining internal security in as many as 13 states during 1973-1974 ..."[11] alone.

Coincident with this build-up of police and para-military power, the Government of India was enacting increasingly repressive laws (e.g., *The Maintenance of Internal Security Act of 1971*) under which people could be detained without trial for indefinite periods. At the same time, the Indian Army was also being used as a direct

---

9. Banerjee, Sumanta. *India's Simmering Revolution: The Naxalite Uprising.* (London: Zed Books Ltd., 1984), p. 275.

10. Ibid.

11. Ibid.

instrument of civil authority in the maintenance of "law and order."

Giving impetus to and, at the same time, reflecting concern about the possibility of rural violence in India was (as noted earlier in this essay) the widely circulated, but unpublished, report in 1969 by the Home Ministry entitled "The Causes and Nature of Current Agrarian Tensions." That report raised the specter of widespread rural unrest and violence resulting less from organized peasant movements led by political parties than from peasants' own perceptions of a widening gap between an affluent minority in the countryside who enjoyed secure rights in land and the large and growing numbers of marginal landholders, sharecroppers, and landless laborers. While emphasizing that peasants did not then appear to have the capacity to sustain agitations that would threaten established authority, the report made plain that peasants did show an increasing ability to perceive the need for change in their condition and to take direct action in their own interests. In this context, the states were urged to take remedial steps (e.g., the inclusion of zones of real and potential unrest in the then fashionable Comprehensive Area Development Program and the quick implementation of land reforms already enacted into law) designed to reduce tensions among rural "haves" and "have-nots," and to stabilize the countryside. Needless to say, with political power in the states in the hands generally of affluent landholders, it could not have been expected that vigorous steps would in fact be taken to reduce tensions by addressing directly the needs of the rural poor. One could not have expected the Congress Party, in particular, to take actions that might threaten the economic roots of the authority and power of some of its own leaders.

There is no reason in the 1980s to believe that the Government of India is any less willing than in the late 1960s and early 1970s to use its police and military power against peasant movements. Indeed, the case can be made that the Government of India has shown an increasing propensity to suggest that those who engage in violent behavior in rural areas are by definition either "Naxalites" (e.g., in Bihar) or terrorists (e.g., in the Punjab). This propensity is reminiscent of the labeling process in the United States by which guerrillas in Central America are by popular definition "leftist guerrillas" -- as if all such anti-government forces have an obvious and explicit ideological patina. Such a labeling process is dangerous for those who rule as well as for those who are fitted with the labels of prevailing stereotypes. The danger for those who rule results from their substitution of crude stereotypes for analysis that would undoubtedly reveal that guerrillas' motivations are extremely diverse and difficult to categorize. The danger for those who are crudely labeled and stereotyped comes from the fact that the process absolves those in power from a need to understand the complex causes and nature of rural unrest. And, when absolved of the need to understand, those who rule can justify easily the most repressive action against whole groups of undifferentiated people -- now clearly identified uniformly as "enemies of the state" unworthy of understanding or respect.

This process continues to be characterized by legislation (e.g., the 1985 *Terrorist and Disruptive Activities Act*) that threatens to erode further peoples' individual rights and freedoms. But, in a sharp departure from the past, we do not hear in the 1980s of sensitive analysis within Government of the "causes and nature of terrorist activities." Instead of reflective concern that might lead to remedial actions, we too frequently see the quick mobilization of repressive counter-force.

Meanwhile, we wonder whether it can be taken for granted that the Indian Army can be used repeatedly in operations against civilians without suffering a gradual deterioration in morale and without risking its politicization. It would seem only a matter of time before segments of India's military become susceptible to political indoctrination and direction. It must be remembered that the lowest paid *jawans* (ordinary soldiers) are themselves drawn mainly from various strata of peasant families. One wonders how such men will react in the days ahead when called upon to quell agrarian unrest by using force on people with whom they identify.

The Reliability and Discipline of India's Military

It is a striking fact that India now possesses one of the world's strongest and most modern armies. This is a consensus view even among military attaches of several nations, including the United States, who make it their business to become informed about the armies of nations to which they are assigned.

That the Indian Army is a modern army was amply demonstrated in January, February and March of 1987 when it held war games in western India which were said to have been as large as those conducted customarily by NATO forces in Europe. The exercises tended to confirm publicly what had long been known: that the Indian Army is one of the best in the world.[12] As Steven Weisman of *The New York Times* reported, quoting a Western diplomat, "This is a modern army, fully competent for any mission, easily as good as the Chinese, the Koreans or the French."[13]

Without much fanfare, following the Sino-Indian border war of 1962, the Government of India has invested heavily in its military and now maintains a force of at least 1.1 million men, increasingly well-equipped with modern Soviet and Western weapons and advanced electronic systems. It has also strengthened its already impressive indigenous weapons systems' production capacity, and will spend nearly 20 percent of its budget in 1987 ($7.9 billion) on the military. And, the clear prospect is that military expenditures will continue to grow in the 1980s. It has been reported that expenditures are to increase by 25 percent in 1988.[14]

---

12. The exercises also created great, if transitory, tension in the subcontinent. Pakistan considered the "games" sufficiently provocative to mobilize its troops on its border with India. At one point in January of 1987, there were said to be 340,000 men facing each other "... along a 250 mile border from the central deserts to the northern mountains, and there was talk on both sides of an accidental war breaking out." [See Steven R. Weisman's article "On India's Border, a Huge Mock War," in *The New York Times*, (March 6, 1987), p. 3.]

13. Ibid.

14. Ibid.

If the Indian Army in the 1980s is correctly perceived as a powerful, modern force -- the clearly dominant force in the South Asia region in conventional warfare, it may be much more than that in the days ahead.

Even those who talk about the decay of political, administrative and judicial institutions in modern India tend to suggest that the Indian Army is the last institution of the British Raj to maintain standards of efficiency, discipline and professionalism. Indeed, the Indian Army frequently has been described in glowing terms not only as a strong and disciplined fighting force, but also as an institution capable of contributing to India's development as a nation.[15]

It must be emphasized that the Indian Army has had an exemplary record of aloofness from politics and political intrigue. And, the tradition of tight civilian control of the military is a part of the British legacy that the Government of India has sought to retain. This tradition is said to persist in 1988 -- notwithstanding events of the post-Independence period that have resulted in considerable tension between civilian and military leaders. There seems to be a remarkable consensus among Indians and Americans who write on the subject that the military in India will remain subservient to civilian control. The following statement, though it originates in 1975, seems typical of the dominant paradigm, even in 1988. "In India, a military intervention seems to be out of the question: our army -- and thank God for it -- for historical reasons, is apolitical and professional and disciplined."[16]

Another part of the British legacy is the perception of the army as a "... final line of defense for internal security."[17] British recruitment was designed to ensure

---

15. See, for example, Cohen, Stephen P. *The Indian Army: Its Contribution to the Development of a Nation.* (Berkeley: University of California Press, 1971).

16. Manekar, D.R. *A Revolution of Rising Frustrations.* (Delhi: Vikas Publishing House Private Ltd., 1975).

17. Cohen, Stephen P. *The Indian Army: Its Contribution to the Development of a Nation.* p. 54.

that the army would be a secure instrument, when needed, to back civil authority. It was entirely consistent with this perception of the Indian Army that the British used it in support of local police against Indian civilians agitating for Independence.[18] It is not surprising then that Indian nationalists were prone to classify the British Army of India as an anachronistic institution of colonial power -- an institution that could be dangerous to Indian democracy when independence was attained. This nationalist perception of the British Indian Army was associated with a kind of natural loathing for those in the army who, while indigenous to India, gave allegiance to the colonial authority. This perception was also associated among some nationalists, particularly those committed to variants of democratic socialism, with the sense that the army was an inegalitarian, caste-bound institution (comprised mainly of recruits who were "classified falsely" as superior because they represented so-called "martial races") unworthy of continuance without drastic reorganization in Independent India.

Against this backdrop, it is worth noting that, following independence, India's civilian leaders, while maintaining some distance from the Indian Army and ensuring its continuing subservience to civil authority, were reluctant for some time to make major changes in the army's traditional organization and structure. Instead of acting on the perception that the army was anachronistic and a potential threat to democracy, the leaders of Independent India were virtually forced by the circumstances of the partition and, after 1959, the border tensions with the People's Republic of China, to rely on the Indian Army, whatever its perceived limitations, to function as a loyal instrument of state policy.

Nonetheless, some critical, civilian initiated adjustments were made in this "institution of tradition." The position of Commander-in-Chief in India was abolished at Independence and was replaced by three separate chiefs of the army, navy and airforce. As Stephen Cohen has noted, this meant that the Chief of the Army was no longer even first among equals. At the same time, steps

---

18. Ibid., p. 170.

were taken to strengthen the civil authority in the Ministry of Defense, and to transform the "Warrant of Precedence" to ensure that civil servants of high rank were given even higher rank in comparison with military officers than their predecessors of the same status had earlier enjoyed. All such steps seem to have been rationalized as enhancing civilian control of the military, and diminishing any tendencies in the military for decision-making outside the administrative frame of that civilian authority.

Probably the most substantial changes in the organization and structure of the Indian Army were initiated during the tenure of V.K. Krishna Menon as Minister of Defence. Menon, a confidant of Jawaharlal Nehru, acerbic tongued and brilliant, repeatedly demonstrated his authority over the military. He widened the base of recruitment of the officer corps, tried to make the military more aware of its social obligations, expanded the indigenous components of defense production, and (with Nehru) intervened even in the minutia of strategic planning and the placement of army units during the border war with China in 1962. While his tenure can be said to have further asserted the civilian control of the military, Krishna Menon's behavior was so politically intrusive that it certainly can be said also to have precipitated tensions within the officer corps.

While the Indian Army remains in the 1980s steeped in tradition, distinctive changes have been made in the Army's recruitment, organization, and structure over the last forty years. As a result, the Army is no longer, as it was in the 1950s, continuing to recruit large numbers of Punjabis. Typically, in the 1950s, one-third of the cadet corps at the National Defense Academy came from the Punjab; Delhi supplied fifteen percent; Madhya Pradesh, Madras, Mysore, and Kerala supplied less than five percent each; and West Bengal and Andhra supplied less than one percent of the cadet corps in some years.[19]

After 1962 (following the Sino-Indian border war), the Indian Army quickly doubled in size. Its recruits were increasingly representative of all segments of Indian society. The army ceased to subscribe to the old British

19. Ibid., pp. 183-84.

practice of "class recruitment."[20]   Such recruitment,
beginning in the nineteenth century following the trauma
of the Indian "mutiny" (as the British perceived it), was
designed systematically to favor subsets of soldiers (e.g.,
Sikhs, Punjabi Muslims, Rajputs, Jats, and Dogras) who had
confirmed their loyalty to the British in the crisis of the
mutiny, and could be classified roughly as Aryan or
sub-Aryan "martial races."[21]   And this bias resulted in the
systematic denigration (for purposes of recruitment to the
army) of some groups in India (e.g. Tamils and Telugus
from Madras, and Biharis, who had contributed to earlier
British victories but had mutinied in 1857), and the
elevation of others (e.g., Punjabis and Gurkhas).   Thus, as
Steve Cohen has pointed out, we find the number of
Madras regiments declining from forty in 1862 to eleven in
1914, the number of Punjabi regiments growing from
twenty-eight in 1862 to fifty-seven in 1914, and the

---

20. The British policy of "class recruitment" meant that class regiments,
comprised of the same ethnic or caste group and drawn from British
designated "marshall races," were systematically developed. This led to what
has been called the "Punjabization of the Indian Army." In 1974, the
Government of India announced a new recruitment policy fixing proportions
for new recruits by population percentages in the various states. The new
policy set the percentage for the Punjab at only 2.5 percent. However, it
seems that this recruitment policy has never in fact been vigorously
implemented. [This is the view set forth in a public lecture by retired
General of the Indian Army, T.S. Arora, at the Tandoor Restaurant, June 19,
1987, Washington, D.C.] Whether intended consciously to diminish the
numbers of Sikhs in the Indian Army or not, the decision of the central
government in 1974 to establish new criteria for national recruitment to the
army could only contribute to the Sikhs' sense of alienation from the
authority and policies of the Centre.

21. The non-scientific basis for the theory of the "martial races" was
enunciated in the 1920s by Lieutenant-General Sir George MacMunn in his
book, *The Martial Races of India*. The book was republished in 1979.
[MacMunn, Sir George. *The Martial Races of India*. (Delhi: Mittal
Publications, 1979).] For a scathing contemporary reference to this work, see
M.J. Akbar's *India: The Siege Within*. (Harmondsworth, Middlesex, England:
Penguin Books, Ltd., 1985), p. 166.

number of Gurkha regiments growing from five to twenty in the same period.[22]

The old recruitment biases are clearly less operative in modern India. While some homogeneous units of Sikhs and Gurkhas continue to exist in the 1980s, the modern standards emphasize the formation of "mixed" regiments (e.g., a Rajput regiment in which some Bengalis are enrolled as Rajputs in name only) and "totally mixed" regiments (e.g., a Madras regiment comprised mainly of people drawn from several Southern states, and including Christians, Hindus, and Muslims).[23] While precise data on the current (1988) composition of the army has not been released by the Government of India, it appears that single caste units are in the 1980s a thing of the past. Thus, whereas a Mahar regiment had earlier in British India been comprised of "untouchable" Mahars, in today's India it might consist either of a variety of castes (including Mahars) or, at least, other "untouchables", e.g., Chamars. In any event, it is obvious that the Indian Army can no longer be classified as being recruited mainly from groups said to be among the "martial races" of India. Indeed, the Government of India has progressively sought to ensure that the army is representative of all segments of Indian society.

Writing in 1971, Stephen P. Cohen suggested that the army's traditional use in support of civil authority was diminishing as para-military forces were created to perform that function in Independent India.[24] But, the growth of para-military forces notwithstanding, this can no longer be said in the 1980s. Indeed, when the army was called to action in the Punjab in 1984, All India Radio -- citing the still operative language of the military manual left behind by the British -- made plain that the army was being employed in aid of the civil authority. There is obvious irony in this use of the Indian Army by the Government of

---

22. Cohen. *The Indian Army: Its Contribution to the Development of a Nation.* p. 44.

23. Ibid., p. 188.

24. Ibid., p. 194.

The Republic of India for purposes within its own borders that are virtually coincident with those of the British colonial power in an earlier era.

While the use of the Indian Army in Operation Blue Star (marked by forced entry in June of 1984 into the complex of the Golden Temple in Amritsar) was indeed consistent with the use of the army to bolster civilian authority in colonial times, it is a bench mark event of historic proportions in modern India. Precisely because the army was thus used against a subset of dissident civilians in a bloody engagement within a sacred place of worship (however much that place had been transformed into an armed camp), it will be difficult for many years to come for those who rule India to escape this precedent and to establish a new tradition by which the army is seen less as an instrument of "internal security" than as a force protecting India mainly from external threats.

The "bench mark" quality of Operation Blue Star notwithstanding, it has been evident for some time that the role of the military in independent India has been extensive -- and not only because of external threats, real or imagined. The army has been used persistently as a coercive instrument of state policy in the maintenance of law and order in modern India. It was "... called out in aid of the civil power on no less than 476 occasions ..." in the ten years from 1961 to 1970 and deployed in aid of civil authority 376 times in the period from 1975-1985.[25] With the seemingly progressive deterioration of civil authority and the use of local police for partisan ends, it has become acceptable in India to perceive the army as "... the only force that can be relied upon to act impartially."[26]

This favorable perception of the army as an impartial, apolitical instrument of state policy has been so persistent and widespread within and outside India that few persons are prepared to assert that the army, in the days ahead, could be transformed either into a partisan instrument of

---

25. Banerjee. *India's Simmering Revolution.* p. 276.

26. Ram, Mohan. "Frightening Foretaste." *Far Eastern Economic Review.* (May 9, 1985), p. 34.

those who rule or into a "rogue elephant" capable of acting on its own to subvert civilian authority and take power. It has been the conventional wisdom of knowledgeable persons that the Indian military would continue to be a stable and predictable institution in modern India -- indeed, a deterrent to regional fragmentation, separatist tendencies and secession. As noted at the outset of this discussion, even those who are prepared to suggest that other institutions of authority in India have been weakened, or are in decay, still tend to see the military as an exemplary institution, worthy of continuing trust, and capable of maintaining the highest standards of professionalism.[27] Such a perception of the military in India cannot easily be dismissed. There is no clear evidence that the military already has been politicized or might be disposed to take by itself an independent course. Moreover, it can be argued that the changes that have been effected in the recruitment and organization of the army since independence help to ensure that the army is so comprised of heterogeneous elements from the whole of India that a military coup would be virtually impossible. From this perspective, it is unimaginable, for example, that a senior officer in New Delhi (together with units commanded by him) could revolt against the civil authority and expect his fellow officers elsewhere in India to go along.

I am not so certain that this popular and professional assessment of the Indian Army is accurate in 1988 -- or will be accurate in the future. The more the army is used for internal security and domestic political purposes, the more likely the day will come when it is politicized.[28] Moreover, the persistent inability of local authority to rely on the police to address civil disturbances makes it likely

---

27. This perception of the Indian military was emphasized, for example, by Mark Tully, the long-time correspondent of the BBC in India, speaking on October 27, 1986 at the "Seminar on Contemporary South Asia" at Queen Elizabeth House, Oxford University, Oxford, England.

28. In this context, see Elkin, Jerrold F. and Ritezel, W. Andrew. "Military Role Expansion in India." *Armed Forces and Society*, Vol. II No.4. (Summer 1985), p. 490.

that the military will continue in the foreseeable future to be employed as a last resort in "police actions" against civilians. The failure of the New Delhi police to cope with the anti-Sikh riots following Mrs. Gandhi's assassination in October of 1984[29] and the Centre's subsequent need on that occasion to employ the army to restore order cannot be described as isolated and atypical events in modern India -- even if the rioting on this occasion was the worst since that associated with the division of the subcontinent in 1947.

As noted earlier, the willingness of India's civilian leaders to employ the military in support of the civil authority -- as did the British colonial rulers before them -- has been persistent for many years. This willingness to use the military in aid of civil authority was brought to a crescendo by Mrs. Gandhi herself, given her penchant for using any means at her disposal to secure her own authority and to assert the power of the Centre over the states. In her watch precedents were set (including the first use of the army to direct the affairs of an Indian state since 1947) that can have long-term implications for the future of civilian-led, democratic government in India.

If, in the days ahead, there is a progressive willingness of the Government of India to accommodate pressures for forms of regional autonomy (as when Rajiv Gandhi reached an accord with secessionist insurgents in Mizoram in 1986, accepted the election of a non-Congress government in Mizoram in 1987, and negotiated accords with militant Gurkhas and Tripura insurgents in 1988), the use of the military to assert civil authority may gradually diminish. This could institute a healthy trend -- one in which the military's coercive power is scarcely used to preserve the "unity" of India.

It is equally possible, however, that civilian authority in the days ahead will conceive of no better means of preserving internal security and the unity of India than by force of arms exercised by the military. If this were to become the *modus operandi* of civilian authority, that

---

29. See, for example, Steven R. Weisman's report on the findings of the Ranganath Misra Commission in the *New York Times*, (February 24, 1987), page 7, entitled "Inquiry Faults Police in '84 India Riots."

authority should not be surprised if its military instrument ceases to maintain its disciplined, professional image and its apolitical role in the country. Clearly, a weak civil authority -- an authority uncertain of its capacity to cope by non-military means with those in the Punjab who agitate for an independent Khalistan, those in north eastern India (e.g., the Nagas) who continue to press for forms of regional autonomy, those contributing to pockets of agrarian unrest in Bihar, and those elsewhere who are variously labeled as "terrorists," Naxalites, and "extremists" -- could become more and more dependent on the military. Such a trend toward civilian dependency on the military to deal with a wide range of domestic issues associated with "internal security" would surely, in my view, hasten the day when the military "takes-over" in India. And, the likely scenario of such a take-over would not be that of a *coup d'etat*, but rather one in which the military, either literally or as part of a carefully orchestrated deception, would be asked to intervene in circumstances where civilian authority would make plain publicly that it could no longer maintain constitutional government. Within the context of such a scenario, the army could defend publicly and rationalize its new role on the grounds that it sought nothing more than to preserve and protect the institutions of state that could then in no other way be protected. In fact, of course, such a military take-over could usher in a new era of change profound enough to be defined as "revolutionary" in character and scope.

5

THE PROSPECTS FOR
REVOLUTIONARY CHANGE

THE DEFINITIONAL DILEMMA

The paradox of modern India is that it has been remarkably stable for forty-one years within the frame of its constitutionally established system of governance and, at the same time, torn periodically by the legal and extra-legal agitations of diverse groups within its borders pressing for forms of social, economic and political change. Some of the movements for change (particularly those labeled terrorist, secessionist, extremist, insurgent, and Naxalite by the Government of India itself) have produced events that might be classified as having revolutionary portent: events that seem to be the precursors of revolutionary change. The problem, however, is that we have difficulty knowing when or whether events classified as having "revolutionary portent" will produce a revolution. Revolutions are difficult to identify until they have happened. Generally, we recognize that a revolution has occurred after the fact. Before the fact, even the most astute observers of events having similar properties will label them variously. The lines separating "revolution" from peasant rebellions and revolts, regional insurrections, riots, strikes, anti-colonial struggles of national liberation, etc., are often blurred.

We also have difficulty identifying and specifying the causes of revolutions -- particularly when events that seem causal in the context of what we call a "revolution" in situation "A" do not have the same effect in situation "B".

Not surprisingly then, scholars will debate endlessly the definition of a revolution. For some, what characterizes "... a revolution is a complete overthrow of a government or social system by those previously subject to it, and the substitution of a new government or social system."[1] Within this definitional frame, it can be said that the Russian and Chinese revolutions, because they "Altered in a profound sense the social structures of the societies in which they took place ..."[2] are "classical revolutions."

If we employ the distinction just made, it seems most unlikely that we shall experience in the foreseeable future a "classical revolution" in India -- that is to say, one which replicates the events of either the Russian or Chinese revolutions. This is not to suggest, however, that India will escape "revolutionary change" by some other definition.

THE SEEMING ABSENCE OF CONDITIONS FOR A CLASSICAL REVOLUTION

At first blush, the conditions for a "classical revolution" (having the properties of either the Russian or Chinese revolutions, or some mix of the elements of both of those revolutions) do not seem to exist in contemporary India.

First, there is no one in contemporary India (or, so far as I know, in exile) who can be described as a prospective leader of a revolutionary movement. There is no person (or group of persons) who can be identified as having articulated a revolutionary strategy and having taken the steps needed to mobilize people to fight for goals consistent with effecting a "classical revolution."

Second, there is no established political party (or less formal grouping of like-minded persons) which has conceptualized and tested within Indian conditions a

---

1. Johnson, H.J., J.J. Leach, and R.G. Muehlmann eds. *Revolutions, Systems, and Theories.* (Dordrecht, Holland: D. Reidel Publishing Company, 1979), p. 160.

2. Ibid.

revolutionary message or ideology. Neither is there a contemporary political party which can be classified by its behavior (as distinct from periodic rhetorical flourishes) as a revolutionary party committed to the systematic development of ideas, concepts, or symbols which might be useful in mobilizing people around goals linked to the promotion of a classical revolution.

Among the political parties of India, there is only one which can claim to be a national party. That party, the Congress (I), is a party of vested interests and the status quo -- even though it is capable of accommodating some change within the existing system of governance.

The Communist Party is splintered, faction-ridden, and geographically localized. The Communist Party of India (Marxist) is not at present (if it ever was) a revolutionary party. Its political program is, in its essence, slightly to the right of the British Labor Party. While the CPI-M has been successful in West Bengal in extending its political coverage and regional eminence by establishing a nexus between its urban-based intellectual elite and sections of the peasantry by means of "Operation Barga",[3] the CPI-M message to its constituents in the countryside is not revolutionary in tone or in substance.

The remaining political parties, including the Janata, are essentially regional in character. Their messages are tuned to local interests. Their programs are parochial, rather than national. While they are prepared to challenge the authority and primacy of the central government on many questions, and to press for the devolution of power from the Centre to the states, none can be classified as being committed to revolutionary transformation of the Indian socioeconomic and political systems. None can be said to be committed to the promotion of a classical revolution in India.

Third, even if there were identifiable leaders in India (persons who had articulated a "revolutionary ideology"),

---

3. Operation Barga is, in its essence, a program of tenurial reform. It has involved a *de jure* process by which *bargadars*, or sharecroppers, have been registered as holders of land in their cultivating possession. This has conferred on them more secure rights to land than they had prior to Operation Barga when local landlords could remove sharecroppers at will.

backed systematically by political parties committed to "revolutionary change," whom would they lead? Would they try to mobilize the "rural majority" of "peasants" -- thereby defining "peasants' interests" as if they were homogeneous, when any sophisticated rural analysis confirms that they are not? Would they focus on identifiable groups of potential followers in rural areas (small bands of peasant insurgents, already conveniently classified by the Government of India as "leftist extremists" or Naxalites) in depressed areas of the "Hindi belt" in North India -- thereby ignoring potential followers in South India, or elsewhere in the subcontinent? Would they focus on mobilizing the urban proletariat, discounting the issue of national "numbers" in this category?

Fourth, there is no foreign devil which can be invoked to produce a united front for revolutionary purposes among the diverse peoples of India, even though the "hidden hand" of the Central Intelligence Agency is often invoked by some leaders of the Government of India as a kind of devil symbol to convey the notion that domestic crises have "external" roots. There is no neo-colonial power that can be used to promote a "nationalist upsurge" which could give power and direction to a revolutionary movement. And, in the same vein, there is no "invading army" (as was the case in China prior to its revolution) which might be used by those seeking to promote a revolution to induce people to abandon their attachment to parochial needs and to come together in a united front against a common enemy. Neither is there at present a foreign power capable (by itself) either of destabilizing India or of contributing meaningfully to conditions within India that would lead to a "classic revolution," as we have defined it. This is not to suggest that India's neighbors customarily avoid involvement in Indian affairs. It is evident that Pakistan will, when it can, assist groups in India: for example, Sikhs who are pressing for an independent Khalistan to be carved out of the Indian Punjab and who are engaged in political activities which threaten the stability of the Indian political system. But, Pakistan, in and of itself, is in no position to develop or nurture a broad-based revolutionary movement in India -- even if there are some in Pakistan who might welcome the opportunity to do so. Similarly, it is difficult to foresee how any other of India's immediate neighbors, including China, could nurture within India a broad-based revolutionary movement -- even if they chose, on occasion, to meddle in India's internal affairs.

Moreover, the long-term interests of both the Soviet Union and the United States in India are likely to be coincident, rather than divergent: neither of the super powers can be interested in changes in the subcontinent that would overturn the present Government of India. It is, at least, difficult to anticipate the time when either of the super powers would have reason to work consciously to destabilize India or to contribute to the development of movements within India having revolutionary potential.[4]

In sum, I see no basis for anticipating a classic revolution in India: one incorporating features of twentieth century revolutions in Russia and China. No one at present can be identified in India who would lead such a revolution. There is no contemporary political party in India to give ideational content and direction to such a revolution. And, it is difficult to conceptualize how and why "outsiders" -- either neighboring states or the super powers -- would promote such a revolution.

Notwithstanding these observations concerning the absence of conditions in India that might be considered conducive to the promotion of a classic revolution, the case can be made that India has already been "living in a revolution"[5] having its own origin, definition, and contextual characteristics.

---

4. The Soviet Union has done its best to maintain its distance from those in India, outside of government, who look to the USSR for tangible support. Moreover, the Soviet Union can have no illusions that its active support would somehow enhance the strength of, or give revolutionary fervor to, the Communist Party of India.

5. The phrase "living in a revolution" is drawn consciously from an essay by Professor M.N. Srinivas entitled "On Living in a Revolution." While my thoughts on this subject are my own, they have been in some measure stimulated by the Srinivas essay. For the full text of Srinivas's "On Living in a Revolution," see pages 4-24 in *India 2000: The Next Fifteen Years*, a book edited by James R. Roach and published in 1986 in Riverdale, Maryland, by The Riverdale Company, Incorporated.

THE EXPERIENCE OF
"LIVING IN A REVOLUTION"

At one level of analysis, it can be said that India has been "living in a revolution" for the last thirty-six years. From this perspective the promulgation in 1952 of *The Constitution of India* was itself a revolutionary act: the sudden imposition by an English-speaking minority of governing elites of twentieth century social, economic and political values on the diverse peoples of a new state in which an illiterate majority still lived in accordance with age-old values borne of radically different traditions.

It is one of the ironies of India's modern history that her Founding Fathers, an essentially conservative lot, articulated the need for revolutionary change in India, and gave legitimacy to such change in various documents of state, including the Constitution and the various Five Year Plans. The Founding Fathers endorsed national goals antithetical to the existing social, economic and political order. Early in the history of the new republic, they suggested the need for profound changes in the structure of Indian society. The proposed changes -- for example abolishing "untouchability" -- were of a magnitude sufficient to call them "revolutionary" when contrasted with the traditional norms of behavior then operative in India.

Broadly stated, India's governing elites attempted to work a revolution by non-violent, democratic means. They assumed that economic development (defined vaguely within the framework of Fabian socialist ideals, and nurtured by the state), would ensure that India's economy was radically transformed[6] and its social system made more egalitarian.[7] They assumed, also, that India's new political system, based on a Western model, would buffer the shocks of radical

---

6. The assumption was that there would be sustained economic growth derived, in part, from the introduction of new technology in capital intensive industries; semi-feudal institutions in the agrarian sector would be abolished -- conferring thereby new incentives for production on the peasantry.

7. It was assumed that free elections with unrestricted adult franchise and the ending of discriminatory practices based on "caste" would help to ensure that progressive social change would be a by-product of economic progress.

economic and social change: making plain to the diverse peoples of India that all citizens -- irrespective of their status at birth, their religious beliefs, their ethnicity and cultural preferences -- could expect equal treatment under law.

It should surprise none of us that Independent India, having articulated revolutionary goals, should have had difficulty attaining them over the last forty-one years. Neither should it surprise us if there exists today growing awareness within India, among all kinds of constituencies, that profound gaps exist between the goals first articulated and present achievements. The existence of such "gaps" will increase tensions in any society -- suggesting to some that too much change has been contemplated and attempted, and to others too little. In other words, the perceived gaps between articulated goals and actual achievements get the attention of people who are threatened by the prospect of change and of those who are eager to promote it. This in turn can contribute to political tensions and unrest: some of it contained within existing political institutions and some of it threatening the existence of those institutions.

Given India's official commitment to programs of economic development having revolutionary content, it was inevitable that those programs would be offensive to some and welcomed by others. For example, there could be no easy agreement across the boundaries of a segmented, plural society when, in order to give substance to "revolutionary ideals," the Government of India took steps to ensure that there would be "reserved places" in institutions of higher education for persons of historically low social and economic status. Providing reserved places in universities for "scheduled castes and tribes" threatened the very people who traditionally have held power in India, and from whom the governing elites have been drawn. To implement seriously a policy designed to provide reserved places for scheduled castes and tribes was to alienate a subset of persons whose commitment to "revolutionary change" in the Indian social system was based, at best, on the questionable "Nehruvian assumption" that India could establish a democratic, socialist society within which traditional elites (including Kashmiri Brahmans) would somehow continue to occupy the apex positions of authority and power.

On the other hand, for the government to implement a program designed to provide reserved places for scheduled castes and tribes was also to convey unprecedented hope of further change in status and economic opportunity to millions of people who, traditionally, had existed as marginal participants in the Indian socioeconomic system. Thus, any program designed to provide new opportunities for long-denigrated persons (even one pursued with sometimes less than revolutionary zeal) would have predictable political consequences. Such a program would engender concern among those who feared its effects would erode their traditional status, and who therefore would work to thwart such change. Such a program would, at the same time, produce concern among those endorsing change at an accelerating rate that the promise of such change might not continue to be forthcoming. I believe that this example illustrates the difficulty of "living in a revolution" -- pursuing revolutionary goals which will be resisted by some and supported by others. Pursuing revolutionary goals in a traditional, inegalitarian, plural society will have predictable effects: passions will be aroused and played out in various ways -- not excluding ways that threaten the stability of the existing order.

Neither could there be widespread understanding among the segmented peoples of India when the Government of India failed, for example, to ensure the implementation of agrarian reforms, and especially land reform, in the Indian states: thereby turning its back on its own "revolutionary" commitment to transform radically the traditional hierarchy of interests in land, and to establish in modern India the basis for a more egalitarian agrarian society. The mere threat of such reforms frightened landlords, themselves members of or allied with the ruling elite. They could not accept gracefully the prospect of any changes in the traditional agrarian system, if such changes altered, or threatened to alter, their inherited status and power. And, peasant cultivators (including landless agricultural laborers and sharecroppers) would ultimately be disappointed, if they dared to harbor the notion that land reforms, as finally enacted in the Indian states, would convey new rights and status on them. This example also illustrates the difficulty

of "living in a revolution;" not pursuing revolutionary goals
(already enunciated) in a traditional, inegalitarian, plural
society will have predictable effects: passions will be
aroused among those who believe that the goals should
have been pursued with vigor, and among those who reject
even the articulation of revolutionary goals, and argue that
maintenance of the *status quo* serves, by definition, the
"national interest" because it serves their interests.

The processes identified above, as well as similar
processes, have aroused passions and produced tensions
within the social and economic systems of modern India.
Such processes confirm that change in a society is taking
place, and is also being resisted.   Such processes also
establish what I am calling here the preconditions for
further change -- possibly revolutionary change of a kind
not likely to be promoted within existing institutions.

What is striking about these processes is that they
affirm the legitimacy of revolutionary goals in modern
India.   They suggest also that revolutionary ferment in
modern India, if and when it occurs, will be rooted in the
"language of revolution" enshrined without introspection
(indeed, almost unwittingly) by her Founding Fathers in
documents of state.   And, revolutionary change, if it takes
place, will result less from the calculated actions of
revolutionary leaders or political parties than from the
gradual growth of awareness among increasing numbers of
people that their interests and needs are not being fulfilled
quickly enough within the existing political and economic
order.

ESTABLISHED "PRECONDITIONS"
FOR REVOLUTIONARY CHANGE

We have suggested above that India's experience of
"living in a revolution" has helped to establish and shape
some of the preconditions for further change -- possibly
even revolutionary change by means not yet experienced in
India.   These "preconditions" derive from processes that
can be traced to government programs broadly linked to
revolutionary goals embedded in India's commitment to
economic development, from government initiatives designed
consciously to promote social, economic, or political

change, and from processes (e.g., population growth) that
are, essentially, independent of government.

Preconditions Associated
with Rapid Population Growth

Among the preconditions that have been established for
further change in India (including possibly revolutionary
change by means not yet experienced), none is greater in
significance than that derived from rapid population growth
in the period from 1947 to the present. In that period,
India's population has more than doubled and, despite
efforts to reduce the rate of growth, it now appears likely
that shortly after the turn of the next century India will
surpass China in its aggregate numbers. This fact alone
threatens the future stability of India. It imposes an
obvious dilemma on any Government of India committed to
economic development within a definitional frame that
embraces, at least implicitly, long-established revolutionary
goals. That is to say, it can never be enough for the
present Government of India simply to sustain economic
growth at a given rate for a given period. It is not
sufficient for economic progress to be measured in
contemporary India only in aggregative terms. There must
be the constant recognition that whatever progress is
achieved must be measured against growing per capita
needs, rising expectations, and even revolutionary promises.
Until the rate of population growth in India is
drastically curbed, India will have to continue to run faster
and faster on its developmental treadmill simply to keep up
with the burgeoning needs and demands of its people. The
dilemma imposed by rapid population growth on those who
govern is made plain when one considers, as we have
earlier noted in this essay, that there may be more people
below the poverty line in India in the year 2000 than there
were people alive in India in 1947. Moreover, it seems
axiomatic that those below the poverty line in the year
2000, especially if they have experienced more than fifty
years of universal adult franchise, will be more capable
than their antecedents of placing demands on the political
economy. It cannot be assumed, of course, that the
poverty and misery of peasants will necessarily lead them

to revolt against those perceived to have created that poverty and misery. As Hannah Arendt once suggested, "Rage is by no means an automatic reaction to misery and suffering as such; no one reacts with rage to an incurable disease or to an earthquake or, for that matter, to social conditions that seem to be unchangeable. Only where there is reason to suspect that conditions could be changed and are not does rage arise."[8] And, as Barrington Moore has said, "There is no guarantee that exploitation, or just plain human misery, will somehow secrete its own antidote."[9]

While it seems clear that a rapid rise in a country's population will not, by itself, become a predictor of revolutionary change, the pressures of increasing numbers on limited agricultural resources have been cited by scholars as an important precondition for agrarian radicalism in numerous countries, including China.[10] "And the potential for agrarian violence is especially high where the effects of too many people on too little land are reinforced by a highly unequal distribution of land among the various strata of the peasantry."[11] These conditions apply within contemporary India.

The rapid growth of population in India has been associated with a worsening man-to-land ratio, the growth of landlessness, and the concentration of landholdings in the hands of a few. This process is one that leads

---

8. Arendt, Hannah. *Crises of The Republic.* (New York: Harcourt Brace Jovanovich, 1972), p. 160.

9. Moore, Barrington, Jr. *Injustice: The Social Bases of Obedience and Revolt.* (White Plains, New York: M.E. Sharpe, Inc., 1978), p. 457.

10. It has been suggested, for example, that the population of China nearly tripled in the period from 1700 to 1850 -- a period leading into the Taiping Rebellion (1848-1865). "And for the sixty years preceding China's first upheavals in the twentieth century, the Chinese population grew at a rate that was probably unprecedented since at least the fourteenth century." [Greene, Thomas H. *Comparative Revolutionary Movements.* (Englewood Cliffs, New Jersey: Prentice Hall, Inc., 1974), p. 122.]

11. Green, Thomas H. *Comparative Revolutionary Movements*, p. 122.

inevitably to disputes over rights in land and to escalating levels of rural violence. It can lead, as it already has in India, to forms of peasant insurgency. It can lead also to counter-insurgency carried out "officially" by police and para-military forces or "unofficially" by *goondas* sponsored by landlords.

Preconditions Associated
with Failed Agrarian Reforms

The failure of agrarian reforms in India (complemented by the tensions in the countryside resulting, in part, from rapid population growth) establishes another precondition for revolutionary change. This failure also confirms the Government of India's inability to fulfill its "revolutionary promise" to its citizens in rural areas that economic progress would be fostered in such a fashion as to ensure not only increases in production, but also improvements in distribution -- providing the basis for a more just and egalitarian society.

Instead of attempting to fulfill its "revolutionary promise," the Government of India chose to focus on a growth-oriented, technology-driven rural development strategy -- a strategy which has been successful if measured only by productivity increases in the aggregate. If judged by its contribution to improvements in the levels of living among all sections of the peasantry, the development strategy which was chosen is grievously flawed. It is a strategy associated with widening income inequality, the growth of landlessness, and an increased concentration of land in the hands of limited numbers of landholders. The failure of agrarian reforms in India, together with the decision to assign higher priority to production increases than to the "revolutionary promise" of distributive justice, has been associated in many regions of India with the growth of what the Home Ministry has called "agrarian tensions" and "rural violence."[12]

---

12. As elaborated in Chapter 3, the Indian Home Ministry in 1969 associated agrarian unrest with what it called "the persistence of serious social and
(continued...)

Agrarian tensions and rural violence persist in contemporary India. The tensions and violence are no longer attributed, as they were in 1969, to the persistence of serious social and economic inequalities. However, if we looked behind the contemporary headlines emphasizing the violent behavior of "left wing extremists," "terrorists," "communalists," etc., I suspect we would find a large proportion of events that could be attributed directly and indirectly to disputes over land in an agrarian society in which widening income and land inequalities are a persistent feature of life.

While it is fashionable in some circles to commend India's considerable achievements since independence in increasing agricultural production in the aggregate, we should not allow those achievements to obscure our vision of the numbers of people in rural India who have experienced widening income and land inequality and whose futures, because they lack secure rights in land, are clouded. The very existence of these people in increasing numbers has revolutionary portent -- even if we cannot now project the scenarios by which they could become mobilized agents of change. As Thomas H. Greene has observed, "It is certainly no accident ... that almost all of the revolutionary movements recorded by modern history have occurred in agricultural societies characterized by an extremely unequal distribution of land. ... Aggregate data

---

12(...continued)
economic inequalities." ["The Causes and Nature of Current Agrarian Tensions." (Government of India, Ministry of Home Affairs, Research and Policy Division, 1969), p. 4.] In recent years, the Government of India has continued to report violent incidents, but has seldom associated those incidents with "agrarian tensions" or "serious social and economic inequalities." Instead, as in the Home Ministry's 1986-1987 annual report on internal security (which does not distinguish formally between incidents that occur in rural and urban areas), violent incidents are attributed -- with negligible socioeconomic analysis -- to "communalism," to "terrorist activities," to "secessionist activities," to "left wing extremists," to "student unrest," to "secessionists and obscurantists," and to "forces which are trying to use religion as a facade to challenge our constitution, our political system and our democratic ethos." [Annual Report. (Government of India, Ministry of Home Affairs, Departments of Internal Security, States and Home, 1986-1987).]

from many countries ... confirm the positive relationship between land inequality and revolutionary potential."[13] While the existence of land and/or income inequality in rural areas will not, by itself, cause a revolution, such conditions seem to raise a society's revolutionary potential.[14] There is, of course, no consensus among scholars concerning when, how, and under what circumstances or conditions peasants will rebel.[15]

Preconditions Associated with Cultural Pluralism

The tensions in India among ethnic, religious, and linguistic groups, and between the central government and

13. Greene. *Comparative Revolutionary Movements.* p. 128.

"In France before 1789, 80 percent of the population were peasants, and while the peasantry owned 40 percent of the land so did less than 2 percent of the population (including the nobility, monarchy, and the Church). ... before the 1905 Russian Revolution, the poorest 10 million peasant families together held no more land than did the 30,000 largest proprietors -- excluding the tsar, Church, and monasteries, whose disproportionate share of the land was even greater. ... In North China in the 1930s, one-third of the population owned more than two-thirds of the land; in the South, less than 5 percent of the population owned between 30 and 50 percent of the land. Prior to the Chinese Communist revolution, 80 percent of China's population were peasants, but only 20 percent of the total population were landowners." [Ibid., pp. 128-129.]

14. For elaboration on this theme, see, for example, Tanter, Raymond, and Manus Midlarsky. "A Theory of Revolution." *Journal of Conflict Resolution,* XI No. 3. (1967), pp. 264-280.

15. There is an extensive literature dealing with rural unrest and the revolutionary potential of peasants under varying conditions. [See, for example: Moore, Barrington, Jr. *Social Origins of Dictatorship and Democracy: Lord and Peasant in the Making of the Modern World,* (1968); Wolf, Eric. *Peasant Wars of the Twentieth Century,* (1969); Paige, Jeffrey. *Agrarian Revolution: Social Movements and Export Agriculture in the Underdeveloped World,* (1975); and Scott, James C. *The Moral Economy of the Peasant: Rebellion and Subsistence in Southeast Asia,* (1976).]

the states, affect political stability, threaten the authority of the central government in a plural society divided administratively into cultural units defined by language, and could provide another precondition for revolutionary change in India. The Government of India at the Centre is increasingly plagued by what it calls "fissiparous, communal and destabilizing forces."[16] These destabilizing forces include what the government calls "terrorist activities" in the Punjab, "extremist activities" in the northeastern region, and "communal disturbances" in various parts of the country.

These destabilizing forces exist in a context where the historic division of responsibilities between the central government and the states of India is the subject of continuing debate. *The Constitution of India* was designed to ensure a kind of "cooperative federalism" within which central authority (i.e., the central government in New Delhi) would be predominant. It was not anticipated at the outset that the states would be encouraged to enlarge on powers conferred on them (within the context of the Constitution) at the expense of the Centre.

However, when it was decided in 1956 to redraw the map of India using the criterion of "linguistic states," the door was opened to all sorts of demands for the devolution of authority from the Centre to the states. These demands have become more strident in the 1970s and 1980s with the growth of regional political parties, factions and groups that play on parochial needs and interests. In a *de jure* sense, as emphasized in Chapter 2, the states' reorganization in 1956 has given legitimacy to all subsequent movements for forms of regional autonomy.

These pressures for forms of regional autonomy do not necessarily threaten the viability of the Indian Union; neither do they provide inevitably a precondition for revolution. However, they do threaten the existing system of governance -- the existing division of authority between the Centre and the states.

In these circumstances, the challenge for the central government will be to respond to the various pressures for

16. *Annual Report*. (Government of India, Ministry of Home Affairs, Departments of Internal Security, States and Home, 1986-1987), Chapt. I, p. 1.

regional autonomy by diverse means. There can be no single policy established to meet different regional needs and demands. The critical task at the Centre will be to resist treating all who agitate for change in their rights and prerogatives as "enemies of the state" -- as persons committed to the dissolution of the Republic of India. The situation cries out for flexible, sensitive, widely differentiated government responses to those who challenge central authority. There must be a clear perception in New Delhi that the Centre's authority need not be confirmed by its capacity to direct or control every dimension of the political process -- particularly in a plural society already organized around linguistic states. There must be a clear perception in New Delhi that its authority in dealing with the states, as well as regional sub-groups within states, is not best established or maintained through the repeated use of coercive means.

The failure of the central government to deal effectively with India's regionally differentiated demands for cultural identity could contribute to the process by which "cultural cleavages" become progressively more threatening to the maintenance of the existing system of governance in India and, in the process, become a precondition for revolutionary change.[17]

Preconditions Rooted
in Weak Civilian Authority

In the 1980s, the Government of India is led by a party, the Congress (I), that, despite its Parliamentary majority, is neither dominant nationally nor, it seems, capable of articulating a vision of the future that will contribute to the establishment of a consensus that bridges the divisions among the diverse peoples of the subcontinent. Those who rule at the Centre seldom give

---

17. Separatist movements, which have proliferated in many parts of the world during this century, can be quite powerful. It has been argued that "... the number and fervor of their supporters is probably much larger than that behind any movement based on revolutionary working-class consciousness." [Moore. *Injustice: The Social Bases of Obedience and Revolt.* p. 484.]

expression to the "revolutionary ideals" that are embedded in the Constitution and other documents of state, and often seem uncomfortable about "living in a revolution." Instead of accepting the notion that political ferment is an inevitable concomitant of the changes (social, economic and political) that derive from economic development, those who rule seem disposed increasingly to value "stability" over "change," and therefore to give primacy to the maintenance of "law and order."

The government at the Centre seems, at times, to have a "siege" mentality. Where there is political ferment, the central government sees "left wing extremists," "terrorists," and other "destabilizing forces." Accordingly, it has taken steps in recent years to enlarge on its constitutional powers and prerogatives as a means of bolstering its authority -- as a means of ensuring from its perspective the Centre's capacity to preserve and protect the "unity and integrity" of the Republic. It has rushed new laws, for example, *The Terrorist and Disruptive Activities (Prevention) Act, 1985*, through Parliament without debate. It has taken steps to strengthen its police and para-military forces.[18]

Both those in power and those in opposition increasingly wonder aloud about the appropriateness of the system of governance imposed on India by the Founding Fathers. It is uncertain in the days ahead whether a common definition of national purpose (which may be essential to the maintenance of a constitutional system in a democracy) will emerge to support the Constitution as it now exists. Such a consensus could founder as the division of authority between the Centre and the states is contested in the political arena.

There is a progressive erosion of ordinary peoples' confidence in the capacity of the government to administer effectively its own programs within the existing system of

---

18. For example, in May of 1985, the Government sanctioned twelve additional battalions of its Central Reserve Police Force (CRPF). This is one of the units "... meant to reinforce the State Police Forces in the event of large scale civil disturbances." [*Annual Report*. (Government of India. Ministry of Home Affairs, Departments of Internal Security, States and Home, 1986-1987), Chapter III, p. 12.]

governance. Public confidence in those who rule and in the institutions of state is strained. What is more, it would appear from their behavior that those who rule lack confidence themselves that the system of governance can function effectively -- except when bolstered by coercive measures exercised by the police, the para-military forces and the military.

All this suggests that another precondition for revolutionary change may have been established in contemporary India -- a precondition derived from the seeming weakness of civilian authority, citizens' doubts about the capacity of the system of governance to meet diverse needs, and the propensity of those who rule to confirm their authority and power by coercive or violent means exercised by the police, the para-military and the military.[19] This is not to suggest, as a Marxist might, that "a revolutionary situation" now exists in India, or, if such a situation did now exist, that it would necessarily develop into a revolution. However, if revolutions have been preceded historically by the disintegration of political systems (signaled by governments' inability to function properly and citizens' doubts about the effectiveness and legitimacy of those governments), the situation in contemporary India is, at least, one that portends change in the existing system of governance.

Having now enumerated and discussed a number of preconditions for revolutionary change that we believe have been established in India, we ask, "What are the prospects for such change in India?"

---

19. It may well be, as Hannah Arendt once observed, that as power declines in a regime, there is a temptation for leaders to substitute violence for power: "... every decrease in power is an open invitation to violence -- if only because those who hold power and feel it slipping from their hands, be they the government or be they the governed, have always found it difficult to resist the temptation to substitute violence for it." [Arendt. *Crises of The Republic.* p. 184.]

THE PROSPECTS FOR
REVOLUTIONARY CHANGE

We have suggested that the prospects for a classical revolution (as defined earlier in this chapter) are negligible in contemporary India.

We have argued also that India has both been "living in a revolution" and establishing the preconditions for some kind (or kinds) of revolutionary change.

The prospects seem good that we shall witness in the not-too-distant future some kind of revolutionary change in India -- one defined to include profound change in the system of governance; the severe amendment or effective dissolution of the existing constitution; the transformation of institutions of state governance that have given meaning and substance to that constitution; and substantial shifts in the directions of social, political and economic policy.[20]

There is now need for a note of caution. As we look toward the future of India, it is important to avoid joining the extreme pessimists who have in the past predicted that India would not persist as a viable state -- that it would break-up or simply fall apart. India (even if it experiences profound shocks or "revolutionary change" along lines of the scenario I have earlier sketched) will persist within its current geography as a plural society comprised of people whose languages, religions, histories and cultures both unify and divide. A *consensus universalis* will not automatically emerge in such a society, whatever its system of governance. Therefore, India may well continue in its present fractious mode (replete with tensions that spill over into violent episodes, regionally differentiated) for many years to come. It is possible that those who rule within the existing system of governance will respond with sensitivity and flexibility to the issues

20. Such a definition of revolutionary change would be consistent with one of Webster's definitions of *revolution*: "a fundamental change in political organization or in a government or constitution." [*Webster's Third New International Dictionary of the English Language*. Gove, Philip Babcock. Editor in Chief. (Springfield, Massachusetts: G. and C. Merriam Co., 1969).] One speculative scenario by which such change could occur in India is outlined in Chapter 4.

that underlie political ferment and outbreaks of violence in contemporary India. It is possible that they will be able to accommodate change within the existing system of governance. Under such conditions, political ferment and violence in India may in the long run be interpreted by historians as "bench marks" confirming mainly that socioeconomic change was taking place -- change that was being promoted by some and resisted by others. After all, India has already managed to "muddle through" forty-one years while "living in a revolution."

In the long run, of course, India, whatever its system of governance, must establish its own best means of living effectively in a segmented, plural society comprised of different ethnic, linguistic, and religious groups, each having its own sense of identity and purpose. It is inevitable that such a society, even when contained within the boundaries of one political unit, will have difficulty establishing and maintaining either a common political will or a consensus definition of economic purpose.

It is also inevitable that such a society will reflect what J.S. Furnivall called "disorganized social demand." This means, in essence, that a plural society may be unable, whatever the system of governance, to express its political and economic needs and interests within the framework of a common definition of purpose. It may instead express only needs and interests that reflect the sectional and regional perspectives of the different groups that make up that plural society. This means that a plural society will, by definition, lack the political economy of a homogeneous society within which conflicts of interest and purpose could be minimal. Instead, the plural society will be characterized by its fractiousness, as different subsets of people try to establish and implement their own agendas for action.

In such a society, economic progress cannot be measured only by a favorable trend rate of economic growth for the political unit which defines the nation-state. Such a measure of progress cannot be sufficient by itself because economic growth can be positive and sustained over time in a plural society while regional and local disparities grow among the diverse subsets of people who make up that society.

In a plural society, economic progress requires (in addition to sustained economic growth measured in aggregative terms) the building over time of a progressively more integrated social and economic system -- one within which a common will and purpose can emerge among people whose backgrounds and interests have been divergent. In the case of India, the long-term need is the building of a society within which people evolve a national consensus that bridges the divisions imposed by language and culture, by caste, by religion, and by economic privilege. The goal, propounded by India's own Founding Fathers, must be to establish, in time, a society that offers to every section of the community and to all parts of the country the fullest opportunity to grow and to contribute to national well-being.[21]

---

21. This goal remains entirely consistent with Vera Anstey's plea nearly sixty years ago: "India is crying out for the persistent and unstinted efforts of her people -- male and female -- inspired by a clear vision of the potentialities of the future, unshackled by bitter and unavailing reflections upon the past, to help her to loosen the bonds of tradition, caste, and superstition. Thus and thus only will she at last attain her rightful position as a free -- and free internally, not only externally -- and prosperous member ... of the World." [Anstey, Vera. *The Economic Development of India*. (London: Longman Green and Company, 1929), p. 487.]

SELECTED
BIBLIOGRAPHY

Ahluwalia, M. "Rural Poverty and Agricultural Performance in India." *Journal of Development Studies*, 14. (1978).
----------. "Growth and Poverty in Developing Countries." World Bank Staff Working Paper No. 309. (1979).
Anstey, Vera. *The Economic Development of India*. (London: Longman Green and Company, 1957).
Arendt, Hannah. *Crises of the Republic.* (New York: Harcourt Brace Jovanovich, Inc., 1969).
Akbar, M.J. *The Siege Within: Challenges to a Nation's Unity.* (Harmondsworth, Middlesex, England: Penguin Books Ltd., 1985).
Austin, Granville. *The Indian Constitution: Cornerstone of a Nation.* (Oxford: Clarendon Press, 1966).
Banerjie, Indranil. "A Startling Sweep." *India Today.* (April 15, 1987).
----------. "The Red Stranglehold." *India Today.* (April 15, 1987).
Banerjee, Sumanta. *India's Simmering Revolution: The Naxalite Uprising.* (London: Zed Books Ltd., 1984).
Bardhan, P.K. "On the Incidence of Poverty in Rural India." *Economic and Political Weekly.* (February, 1973).
Basham, A.L. *The Wonder That Was India.* (New York: Grove Press, Inc., 1954.)
Baxi, Upendra. "Beyond The Denial of Discourse: Violence and Repression in Contemporary India." (Unpublished manuscript, 1986.)
----------. "Reflections on Reservation Crisis in Gujarat." Reprinted from *Mainstream.* (June 8, 15 and 22, 1985).
Beteille, Andre. *Studies in Agrarian Social Structure.* (Delhi: Oxford University Press, 1974).

Bobb, Dilip and Ramindar Singh. "Pakistan's Nuclear Bombshell." *India Today.* (March 31, 1987).

Brass, Paul. "Institutional Transfer of Technology: The Land Grant Model and the Agricultural University at Pantnagar." in *Science, Politics, and the Agricultural Revolution in Asia.* (Boulder: Westview Press, Inc., for the American Association for the Advancement of Science, 1982).

Brown, Dorris D. *Agricultural Development in India's Districts.* (Cambridge: Harvard University Press, 1971).

Bryan, Barry and Gowher Rizvi. *South Asian Insecurity and the Great Powers.* (Houndmills, Basingstoke, Hampshire & London: The MacMillan Company, 1986).

Bryjak, George J. "The Economics of Assassination: The Punjab Crisis and the Death of Indira Gandhi." *Asian Affairs - An American Review.* (Washington, D.C.: Heidret Publications, Spring 1985).

Byres, T.J. "The Dialectic of India's Green Revolution." *South Asian Review*, 5:2. (January 1972).

"Calcutta Diary" by AM. *Economic and Political Weekly*, Vol. XXII No. 9. (February 28, 1987).

Chopra, Pran. *Uncertain India.* (London: Asia Publishing House, 1968).

"Civil Rights: Championing a Cause." *India Today.* (March 31, 1987).

Cohen, Stephen P. *The Indian Army: Its Contribution to the Development of a Nation.* (Berkeley: University of California Press, 1971).

Cummings, Ralph W. Jr. and Susanta K. Ray. *Policy Planning for Agricultural Development.* (Delhi: Tata McGraw-Hill Publishing Company Ltd., 1979).

Dandekar, V.M. and N. Rath. *Poverty in India.* (Poona: Indian School of Political Economy, 1971).

Dantwala, M.L. "The Problem of a Subsistence Farm Economy: The Indian Case." in *Subsistence Agriculture and Economic Development.* Clifton Wharton Jr., editor. (Chicago: Aldine Press, 1969).

Dantwala, M.L. and C.H. Shah. *Evaluation of Land Reforms with Special Reference to the Western Region of India.* (Bombay: Bombay University, 1971).

Darling, Malcolm Lyall. *The Punjab Peasant in Prosperity and Debt.* 3rd edition. (London: Oxford University Press, 1932).

de Toqueville, Alexis. *Democracy in America.* J.P. Mayer and Max Lerner, editors. A New Translation by George Lawrence. (New York, Evanston and London: Harper and Row, Publishers, 1966).

Dorner, Peter. *Land Reform and Economic Development.* (Middlesex, England: Penguin Books, 1972).

Dunn, John. *Modern Revolutions.* (Cambridge: Cambridge University Press, 1972).

Eckholm, Erik. "The Dispossessed of the Earth: Land Reform and Sustainable Development." *Worldwatch,* Paper 30. (Washington, D.C., 1979).

Elkin, Jerrold F. and W. Andrew Ritezel. "Military Role Expansion in India." *Armed Forces and Society,* Vol. II No. 4. (Summer 1985).

Emaneau, Murray B. "India as a Linguistic Area." *Language,* 32. (1956).

Farmer, B.H. *An Introduction to South Asia.* (London and New York: Methuen, 1983).

Frankel, Francine R. *India's Green Revolution: Economic Gains and Political Costs.* (Princeton: Princeton University Press, 1972).

Frykenberg, Robert E. editor. *Land Tenure and Peasant in South Asia.* (Delhi: Orient Longman, 1977).

Furnivall, J.S. *Netherlands India: A Study of Plural Economy.* (Cambridge: Cambridge University Press, 1944).

Gandhi, Rajiv. "Address to the Third Special Session on Disarmament of the United Nations General Assembly." (June 9, 1988) [As printed in *India News*, a publication of the Embassy of India, 2107 Massachusetts Avenue N.W., Washington, D.C.]

Green, Thomas H. *Comparative Revolutionary Movements.* (Englewood Cliffs, New Jersey: Prentice Hall Inc., 1974).

Griffin, K. *The Political Economy of Agrarian Change.* (London: MacMillan, 1974).

Griffin, K. and A.R. Khan. editors. *Poverty and Landlessness in Rural Asia.* (Geneva: ILO, 1977).

Gupte, Pranay. *Vengeance: India After the Assassination of Indira Gandhi.* (New York: W.W. Norton and Company, 1985).

Harrison, Selig S. *India: The Most Dangerous Decades.* (Princeton: Princeton University Press, 1960).

Hart, Henry C. editor. *Indira Gandhi's India: A Political System Reappraised.* (Boulder: Westview Press, 1976).

Hazarika, Sanjoy. "India and Tribal Guerrillas Agree to Halt 8-Year Fight." *The New York Times.* (August 13, 1988).

Hegde, Ramakrishna. "The Emergence of Two Indias." *Business Standard.* (Bombay. January 8, 1987).

Herring, Ronald J. *Land to the Tiller: The Political Economy of Agrarian Reform in South Asia.* (New Haven: Yale University Press, 1983).

Hirschman, A.O. and M. Rothschild. "The Changing Tolerance for Income Inequality in the Course of Economic Development." *Quarterly Journal of Economics,* 87. (1973).

India, Government of. Administrative Reforms Commission. *Report of the Study Team on Agricultural Administration.* Annexures, Volumes I and II. (Delhi: Manager of Publications, 1967).

----------. Ministry of Food and Agriculture. *India's Food Crisis and Steps to Meet It.* (Delhi: Government Press, 1959).

----------. Ministry of Home Affairs, Departments of Internal Security, States and Home. *Report, 1986-1987.* (New Delhi: Government of India, Ministry of Home Affairs, 1987).

----------. Ministry of Home Affairs, National Integration Council. "Minorities in Nation-Building." Proceedings of a seminar organized by the India International Centre with support from the Secretariat of the National Integration Council, Ministry of Home Affairs, Government of India. (New Delhi: India International Centre, 1970).

----------. Ministry of Home Affairs, Research and Policy Division. "The Causes and Nature of Current Agrarian Tensions." (Unpublished Report, 1969).

----------. Planning Commission. *Seventh Five Year Plan.* (New Delhi: Government of India Press, 1985).

----------. *Report on Intensive Agricultural District Programme, 1961-1963.* (New Delhi: Manager of Publications, 1964).

India, Government of. Reserve Bank of India. *Agricultural Productivity in Eastern India. Report of the Committee on Agricultural Productivity in Eastern India.* Volumes I and II. (Bombay: Reserve Bank of India, 1984).

"Indira Gandhi's Bequest." *Economic and Political Weekly,* Vol. XIX No. 44. (1984).

Jannuzi, F. Tomasson. *Agrarian Crisis in India: The Case of Bihar.* (Austin and London: University of Texas Press, 1974).

----------. "India's Rural Poor: What Will Mobilize Them Politically?" Chapter 7 in *Indira Gandhi's India.* Henry C. Hart, editor. (Boulder, Colorado: Westview Press, 1976).

----------. "Land Systems, Economic Growth and Social Justice: The Permanent Settlement Region." Chapter 7 in *Region and Nation in India.* Paul Wallace, editor. (New Delhi, Bombay and Calcutta: Oxford and IBH Publishing Company, 1985).

----------. "Toward Food Security in South Asia." Chapter 7 in *Pursuing Food Security: Strategies in Africa, Asia, Latin America, and the Middle East.* W. Ladd Hollist and F. Lamond Tullis, editors. (Boulder and London: Lynne Rienner Publishers, 1987).

Jeffrey, Robin. *What's Happening to India?* (London: Macmillan Press Ltd., 1986).

Jha, L.K. "The 11th Govind Ballabh Pant Memorial Lecture." Delivered in New Delhi, India on December 10, 1986, at the India International Centre. Text published in *The Times of India.* (New Delhi, December 31, 1986 and January 1, 1987).

Johnson, B.L.C. *Development in South Asia.* (Harmondsworth, Middlesex, England: Penguin Books Ltd., 1983).

Johnson, H.J., J.J. Leach, and R.G. Muehlmann. *Revolutions, Systems, and Theories: Essays in Political Philosophy.* (Dordrecht, Holland, Boston and London: D. Reidel Publishing Company, 1971).

Kashyap, Subhash C. *The Politics of Power: Defections and State Politics in India.* (Delhi: National Publishing House, 1974).

Kolenda, Pauline. *Caste, Cult and Hierarchy: Essays on Culture of India.* (Meerut: Ved Prakash Vatuk, 1983).

Kothari, Rajni. *Politics in India.* (Delhi: Orient Longman Ltd., 1970).

Kothari, Rajni and Gobinda Mukhoty. editors. *Who Are The Guilty?* (Delhi: People's Union for Democratic Rights and the People's Union for Civil Liberties, 1984).

Krishna, Raj. "The Economic Outlook for India." An unpublished manuscript. A version of the manuscript was published as Chapter 9 in *India 2000: The Next Fifteen Years.* James R. Roach, editor. (Riverdale, Maryland: The Riverdale Company Inc., 1986).

Ladejinsky, Wolf. *Agrarian Reforms as Unfinished Business.* Edited by Louis J. Walinsky. (London: Oxford University Press, 1977).

Leaf, Murray J. "The Green Revolution in a Punjab Village." *Pacific Affairs,* LIII 4. (Winter 1980-1981).

----------. "The Punjab Crisis." *Asian Survey,* Vol. XXV No. 5. (May, 1985).

Lohr, Steve. "Inside the Philippine Insurgency." *The New York Times.* (November 3, 1985).

MacMunn, George. *The Martial Races of India.* Republication of a manuscript first published in this century in the 20s. (Delhi: Mittal Publications, 1979).

Mahalanobis, P.C. "Science and National Planning." *The Indian Journal of Statistics,* Vol. 20 Parts 1 and 2. (September 1958).

Manekar, D.R. *A Revolution of Rising Frustrations.* (Delhi: Vikas Publishing House Private Ltd., 1975).

Mann, Harold H. *The Social Framework of Agriculture.* Edited by Daniel Thorner. (Bombay: Tri Printers, 1967).

Maxwell, Neville. "Towards India's Second China War?" *South.* (May, 1987).

Mehta, J.S. *Third World Militarization: A Challenge to Third World Diplomacy.* (Austin: The Lyndon B. Johnson School of Public Affairs, 1985).

Mellor, John W. *The New Economics of Growth: A Strategy for India and the Developing World.* (Ithaca, New York: Cornell University Press, 1976).

Mellor, John W., Uma J. Lele, and R. Sheldon Simon. *Developing Rural India: Plan and Practice.* (Ithaca, New York: Cornell University Press, 1968).

Moore, Barrington Jr. *Injustice: The Social Bases of Obedience and Revolt.* (White Plains, New York: M.E. Sharpe, 1968).

----------. *Social Origins of Dictatorship and Democracy: Lord and Peasant in the Making of the Modern World.* (Boston: Beacon, 1968).

Myrdal, Gunnar. *Asian Drama: An Inquiry into the Poverty of Nations.* (New York: Random House, 1968).

Nayer, Baldev Ray. *Minority Politics in the Punjab.* (Princeton: Princeton University Press, 1966).

Neale, Walter C. *Economic Change in Rural India: Land Tenure and Reform in Uttar Pradesh, 1800-1955.* (New Haven: Yale University Press, 1962).

Noorani, A.G. *Ministers' Misconduct.* (Delhi: Vikas Publishing House Private Ltd., 1973).

Paige, Jeffrey. *Agrarian Revolution: Social Movements and Export Agriculture in the Underdeveloped World.* (New York: Free Press, 1975).

Patel, I.G. "New Economic Policy." Excerpts from the Kingsley Martin Memorial Lecture delivered at Cambridge on November 5, 1986, as published in *The Economic Times.* (Bombay, November 6, 7, & 11, 1986).

Ram, Mohan. "Frightening Foretaste." *Far Eastern Economic Review.* (May 9. 1985).

Rosen, George. *Democracy and Economic Change in India.* (Bombay: Vora and Company, 1966; and Berkeley: University of California Press, 1966).

----------. *Western Economists and Eastern Societies: Agents of Change in South Asia, 1950-1970.* (Baltimore and London: The John Hopkins University Press, 1985).

Ruttan, Vernon W. "The Green Revolution: Seven Generalizations." *International Development Review.* (December, 1977).

Sahni, Sati. editor. *Centre-State Relations.* (Delhi: Vikas Publishing House Private Ltd., 1984).

Scott, James C. *The Moral Economy of the Peasant: Rebellion and Subsistence in Southeast Asia.* (New Haven and London: Yale University Press, 1976).

Sen, Amartya. *Poverty and Famines: An Essay on Entitlement and Deprivation.* (Oxford: Clarendon Press, 1981).

----------. *Resources, Values and Development.* (Oxford: Basil Blackwell Publisher Ltd., 1984).

154

Sethi, J.D. *India's Static Power Structure*. (Delhi: Vikas Publications, 1969).

Singh, Tarlok. *Poverty and Social Change*. 2nd edition. (Delhi: Orient Longman, 1969).

----------. *Towards an Integrated Society: Reflections on Planning, Social Policy and Rural Institutions*. (Westport, Connecticut: Greenwood Publishing Corporation, 1969).

Srinivas, M.N. "On Living in a Revolution." *India 2000: The Next Fifteen Years*. James R. Roach, editor. (Riverdale, Maryland: The Riverdale Company, Incorporated, 1986).

Subramaniam, C. *The New Strategy in Indian Agriculture*. (New Delhi: Vikas Publishing House Private Ltd., 1979).

Sun, Lena H. "Talks to Air Sino-Indian Tension: Armies Said posed on Contested Border." *The Washington Post*. (June 15, 1987).

Sunil, K.P. "The Language Crisis." *The Illustrated Weekly of India*. (June 2, 1985).

"Tamil Guerrilla Groups Call Off Sri Lanka Truce." *The New York Times*. (January 13, 1987).

Tanter, Raymond and Manus Midlarsky. "A Theory of Revolution." *Journal of Conflict Resolution*, XI No. 3. (1967).

"Their Bomb, Our Bomb." *Economic and Political Weekly*, Vol. XXII No. 12. (March 21, 1987).

Thorner, Daniel. *The Agrarian Prospect in India*. (Delhi: Delhi University Press, 1956).

Tully, Mark, and Satish Jacob. *Amritsar: Mrs. Gandhi's Last Battle*. (London: Pan Books Ltd., 1986).

Wallace, Paul. editor. *Region and Nation in India*. (New Delhi: Oxford and IBH Publishing Company, 1985).

Warriner, Doreen. *Land Reform in Principle and Practice*. (London: Oxford University Press, 1962).

Weisman, Steven R. "India's Corner of Misery: Bihar's Poor and Lawless." *The New York Times*. (April 27, 1987).

----------. "Inquiry Faults Police in '84 Riots." *The New York Times*. (February 24, 1987).

----------. "On India's Border, A Huge Mock War." *The New York Times*. (March 6, 1987).

Weisman, Steven R. "Sri Lanka Strains India's Patience: Resistance by Tamil Guerrillas and Colombo to an Accord has New Delhi Uneasy." *The New York Times.* (December 27, 1985).

Weller, Robert P. and Scott E. Guggenheim. *Power and Protest in the Countryside: Studies of Rural Unrest in Asia, Europe, and Latin America.* (Durham: Duke University Press, 1982).

West Bengal. Department of Information and Cultural Affairs. *Left Front Government of West Bengal and Land Reforms.* (Calcutta, 1984).

Wolf, Eric R. *Peasant Wars of the Twentieth Century.* (New York: Harper and Row, 1969).

World Development Report, 1986. A Publication of the World Bank. (Oxford: Oxford University Press, 1986).

World Development Report, 1987. A Publication of the World Bank. (Oxford: Oxford University Press, 1987).

Zinkin, Taya. *Challenges in India.* (London: Chatts and Windus, 1966).

INDEX